THE FOSSIL HUNTER HANDBOOK

WILLIAM POTTER

ARCTURUS

CONTENTS

Introducing fossils — 4
How fossils are made — 6

Chapter 1: Know your fossils — 8

Types of fossils — 8
Geological time — 10
Dating fossils — 12
Fossil sites — 14
Fossil hunter toolkit — 16
Fossil displays — 18
Top 10 fossils — 20

Chapter 2: Plants — 24

Algae — 24
Early land plants — 25
Liverworts — 26
Horsetails — 27
True ferns — 28
Seed ferns — 29
Scale trees — 30
Bennettitales — 31
Conifers — 32
Flowering plants — 34
Fossilized wood — 36
Amber — 37

This edition published in 2025 by Arcturus Publishing Limited

26/27 Bickels Yard, 151-153 Bermondsey Street, London SE1 3HA

Copyright © Arcturus Holdings Limited

All rights reserved. No part of this publication may be reproduced, stored in a retrieval system, or transmitted, in any form or by any means, electronic, mechanical, photocopying, recording, or otherwise, without prior written permission in accordance with the provisions of the Copyright Act 1956 (as amended). Any person or persons who do any unauthorized act in relation to this publication may be liable to criminal prosecution and civil claims for damages.

Author: William Potter
Illustrator: Rhys Jeffries
Design: Tokiko Morishima
Editors: Donna Gregory and Becca Clunes
Design Manager: Rosie Bellwood-Moyler
Editorial Manager: Joe Harris

ISBN: 978-1-3988-4459-9

CH011581US

Supplier 29, Date 0225, PI 00006653

Printed in China

Chapter 3: Invertebrates — 38

Early invertebrates	38
Sponges	39
Corals	40
Bryozoans	41
Graptolites	42
Worms	43
Trilobites	44
Crustaceans	46
Brachiopods	48
Crinoids	49
Bivalves	50
Gastropods	52
Belemnites	54
Nautiloids	55
Ammonites	56
Echinoids	58
Sea stars	59
Chelicerates	60
Insects	62

Chapter 4: Vertebrates — 64

Jawless fish	64
Jawed fish	66
Bony fish	68
Amphibians	70
Early reptiles	72
Turtles	73
Crocodilians	74
Lizards	75
Snakes	76
Ichtyosaurs	77
Pleiosaurs	78
Ptserosaurs	79
Bird-hipped dinosaurs	80
Reptile-hipped dinosaurs	82
Birds	84
Proto-mammals	85
Early mammals	86
Creodonts	88
Carnivorous mammals	89
Horses	90
Large herbivores	91
Marine mammals	92
Primates	93
Hominins	94

Glossary — 96

Introducing fossils

Life on Earth began about 3.7 billion years ago. We know this from studying fossils in the rocks beneath our feet. Preserved as stone, these remains and traces of animals and plants help us to understand the history of life on Earth—its successes, its endings, and its incredible ability to adapt. Fossils provide a unique window on prehistoric life.

In ancient England, fossilized sea urchins (page 58) were called fairy loaves and kept as charms. Vikings displayed them as protective amulets.

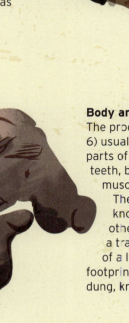

Fossils have been treasured by humankind for millennia, cherished as sacred objects, such as amulets, and worn as decoration. Long ago, they were thought to be gifts from the gods, created by supernatural forces, or shaped by wind or water. By the 1500s, they began to be recognized as the remains of once-living things. The German geologist Georgius Agricola came up with the term "fossil," from the Latin word *fossilis*, meaning "to be dug up." By the end of the seventeenth century the definition of a fossil as evidence of prehistoric life was agreed.

Body and trace fossils
The process of fossilization (page 6) usually preserves just the hard parts of a body or plant, such as teeth, bone, shell, or wood, while muscles and color are lost. These physical remains are known as body fossils. The other main type of fossil is a trace fossil, the impression of a life form. This may be a footprint, a burrow, or even animal dung, known as a coprolite.

Rare finds

While this book aims to encourage the discovery of fossils, most of the fossils featured are rare, and only found in certain parts of the world where ancient rocks are visible. These are collected by experts called **paleontologists**.

The chances of unearthing a dinosaur skull are slim but collecting your own ammonites is entirely possible. Being the first to see the remains of an ammonite locked away for millions of years is always a thrill and may trigger a lifelong interest in paleontology. Fossil hunters have to start somewhere, and all the amazing fossils on display in museums were collected by someone. The next big discovery could be yours!

What is paleontology?
Paleontology means the "study of the ancient." It requires a knowledge of biology and ecology to recognize a life form that died out millions of years ago and to understand its environment. Paleontologists also need a grasp of geology to date layers of rock and sediment, and to have a keen eye for shapes that may be part of an ancient creature, a fossilized bone, shell, or branch. As well as working in the field to locate and collect specimens, paleontologists work in the laboratory, carefully removing fossils from surrounding stone, studying, and categorizing their discovery.

Regular updates
New fossils provide new information on the past. The understanding and registering of fossils is under constant review. Some of the fossils featured in this book have changed classification since their first discovery. Some may do so in the future. Several categorizations are disputed by different experts. New discoveries and new science mean the study of the past is full of surprises.

How fossils are made

Fossilization is a rare occurrence that requires a plant or animal to die and be covered soon afterward. Living organisms are preserved as fossils in several ways. Some are buried beneath layers of sediment and rock and their bones replaced with minerals over thousands of years. Others may be frozen, mummified, or pickled. The most common fossils are those of marine creatures buried on the sea floor.

1. An animal is buried by sediment, such as volcanic ash, silt from rivers, or sand on the seabed, before its body can be scavenged or rot away.

2. All the soft parts of the animal are eaten by other creatures, or else just rot away, leaving only the hard parts like bones and teeth.

3. Water seeps into the animal's teeth and bones, replacing the tissues with dissolved minerals. Over millions of years, these harden into stone.

4. The movement of the Earth's tectonic plates pushes the fossil toward the surface, where wind and water erosion reveals it.

Deep freeze
Mummified mammoths have sometimes been found in preserved in permafrost. Although crushed, the mammoth's flesh, fur, and tusks have been revealed intact as the ancient ice melted.

Trapped in tar
The bones of prehistoric animals, including saber-toothed cats, dire wolves, mammoths, mastodons, and ground sloths, have been preserved in tar such as the La Brea Tar Pits in Los Angeles, USA.

Preserved in amber
Some small creatures, such as insects and spiders, have been preserved in coniferous tree sap, which hardened into amber. The resin protects the finest detail on the creature, though its DNA does not survive intact for long.

CHAPTER 1: KNOW YOUR FOSSILS

In this first chapter, you'll learn the basics of fossil hunting, the equipment you'll need, where to look, and how to identify and display your treasured pieces of prehistory. We'll look at the various types of fossils you may encounter and where in the many millions of years of Earth's past they might have survived from.

Type of fossils

Fossils come in many shapes and sizes, from microscopic traces to flattened imprints to complete dinosaur skeletons.

Petrified fossils
The most common method of fossilization is petrification. This is where the buried hard parts of an organism—the bones, teeth, and shell—are replaced by hard minerals such as silica or calcium carbonate.

Compressed fossils
When the bodies of plants or animals are squeezed by the weight of sediment, rock, or water above them, an imprint can be left in the rock.

Molds and casts
The shape of a skeleton or shell may remain in the rocks once the original material has dissolved away, leaving a mold. This can become filled by sediment, to create a cast.

ON TRACK

Not all fossils are the remains of a creature. Trace fossils are evidence of their movement. They include tunnels dug by prehistoric creatures and footprints left in mud. This preserved theropod print was discovered in coastal rocks in Wales. The depth and location of the prints can tell paleontologists a lot about how the animal moved, how it positioned its weight, and even its walking speed. Tracks of several sauropods together have revealed that these giants traveled in herds.

This trace fossil shows a dinosaur footprint.

This fossil of the small dinosaur *Sinosauropteryx*, discovered in 1996, reveals its coat of short, downy feathers.

FEATHERED FOSSILS

In very rare instances the remains of feathers have survived in fossils. Feathers are made from keratin, which decays more slowly than muscle and flesh. Discoveries in Liaoning, China, have included the appearance of feathers on dinosaurs, including velociraptors. Scientific studies have confirmed the link between theropod dinosaurs and modern-day birds. Chickens are distant relatives of the *T. rex*!

Geological time

The geological history of planet Earth from its formation 4.6 billion years ago to the present day has been divided into intervals, based on events and fossils recorded in layers of rock. The timescale is made up of eons, which are split into shorter eras, then periods. The appearance and evolution of life can be mapped on this timescale. Fossil remains help geologists identify the age of the rocks they are examining.

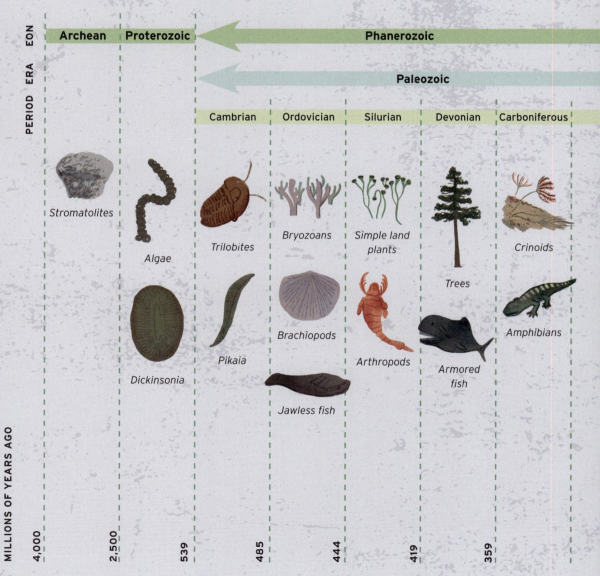

Dating fossils

Paleontologists work out the age of a fossil by comparing it to other fossils found nearby and by using scientific methods to date the rocks above and below it.

Relative dating
Over millions of years sediment, rock, and lava form layers, or strata, on the Earth's surface, with the oldest rocks becoming the deepest. These layers can be identified by examining the different types of rock, deposits of ash from major volcanic eruptions, and any embedded fossilized remains.

Jurassic Period

Triassic Period

Perisphinctes tiziani

Index fossils
Common fossils can be used to estimate the age of layers of rock. These are known as index fossils. These include short-lived creatures such as ammonites, sea urchins, and trilobites. If a fossilized creature is known to have become extinct 190 million years ago, fossils found above it must date from more recent times.

Tropites subbullatus

Relative dating

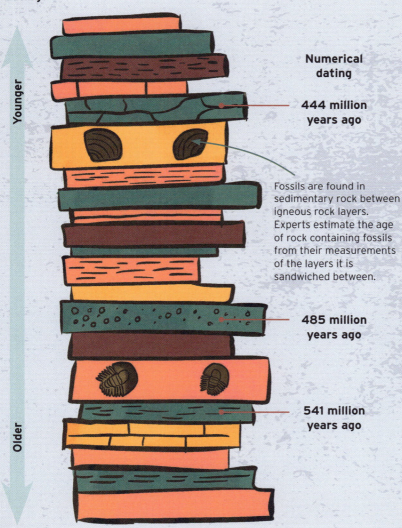

Younger ↕ Older

Numerical dating

444 million years ago

Fossils are found in sedimentary rock between igneous rock layers. Experts estimate the age of rock containing fossils from their measurements of the layers it is sandwiched between.

485 million years ago

541 million years ago

Numerical dating
Minerals in cooled molten rock, known as igneous rock, within the Earth's crust may contain traces of radioactive elements. These are unstable and decay over millions of years, becoming different elements. By knowing the rate of decay and measuring the proportion of elements in the minerals, scientists can work out how long the radioactive elements have been decaying and calculate an age for the rock.

Fossils younger than 60,000 to 80,000 years old, such as human and mammoth bones, can be dated using a method called radiocarbon dating.

Fossil sites

Maps and local knowledge can guide you to sites where you can search for fossils, but make sure you get permission, are well prepared, and conscious of safety.

Fossils are found in sedimentary rock formed when sand and earth are deposited over animal or plant remains by wind or water. Sedimentary rock includes limestone (mostly shell and skeletal remains), shale (hardened clay), and sandstone (eroded rock grains). Over a long period of time, this sedimentary rock hardens. While these rocks are often covered by plant life, some ancient strata can become exposed along coastlines or as the result of quarrying work.

Geological maps

Maps that show the type and age of exposed rocks are hugely useful for fossil hunters. These geological maps use different colors to show the strata found on the surface. Paleontologists looking for dinosaur fossils visit sites where the exposed rock dates from between 250 and 66 million years ago, particularly from the Jurassic and Cretaceous Periods. As dinosaurs were land creatures, their remains are likely to be found close to the shores of ancient lakes and seas. Major sites for dinosaur fossils include the deserts and badlands of North America, Argentina, and China.

Getting permission

Do not assume you can dig for fossils anywhere. Check restrictions and get permission from the site owner or manager before planning your visit. Some areas are privately owned, and others are protected by special laws designed to regulate access to sites that are known to have fossils. Visit the website for the authority that manages the site you're hoping to explore and follow their procedures. If you can't easily find the land owner or manager, contact a local museum or geological society that might be able to point you in the right direction.

Locations

For the best fossil-hunting sites that are open to the public, check online and in libraries, or join a local geological group for an invitation to a field trip.

The coast
Fossils may be found in the gravel on the beach. Cliffs may also contain fossils, but hammering into cliffs can be dangerous. Wearing hard hats and steel-capped boots when fossil hunting near cliffs is recommended, as is being aware of the tide times. Winter months, after high tide, as the seawater recedes, is the best time to go looking for fossils. Every tide brings in new stones. Above the cliffs, scree slopes may also contain rocks with fossils.

Farmland
Fossils may be unearthed on farmland where chalk (soft limestone) is near the surface. You will need the farmer's permission to search in fields, but they may be wiling to allow fossil hunting at certain times of the year.

River banks
Fossils are sometimes washed up along river banks or found in river cliff faces. Searching for fossils here requires care, particularly near deep or fast-running water.

Quarries
With prior agreement, supervised fossil-hunting groups can sometimes investigate quarries, where layers of rock are revealed by commercial digging. Visitors must take the same safety precautions as quarry workers, including wearing hard hats, hi-vis jackets, and steel-capped boots, and following all site-specific safety procedures.

How to spot a fossil

Clues that a rock may contain a fossil include regular lines or patterns like those of a shell. Joining a local fossil tour will help you to find out how to spot fossils in the area. With experience you will be able to recognize the types of rocks that may contain fossils, and unusual rock shapes that are worth investigating.

Fossil hunter toolkit

Here's the basic equipment you'll need to uncover, record, and preserve your fossilized treasures.

Weather wise
The most important gear for a fossil hunter is all-weather wear. Looking for fossils takes time and patience, so be prepared for hot and cold weather, as well as rain and wind. You might want some waterproof shoes if you're hunting for fossils in the shingle and rock pools along the coast or rivers.

Safety concerns
Hard hats, such as those worn by climbers, are a must if you're fossil hunting by cliffs or in a quarry. These offer some protection from falling stones but not large rocks, so stay alert.

> **THINK BEFORE YOU REMOVE FOSSILS**
>
> **Take photos**
> Once a fossil has been removed from its location, a lot of the most important information about it is lost forever. Take good photos showing the fossil and its surrounding layers of rock. Only remove a fossil if you are sure you have permission and that it is not of special interest to science. If in doubt, check with a local museum or university before removing any fossils.

 ## A keen eye

When it comes to finding fossils, your eyes are your best tools. Most fossils are found lying on the ground, not through breaking rocks. Spotting unusual shapes and knowing the signs of a fossil are key skills.

Backpack
To protect and carry home any precious finds, you'll need a sturdy bag. Your finds might be muddy or sandy, so pack some plastic bags to wrap them in.

Hammer and chisel
For breaking into rocks, a hammer should have a wide head and be light enough to use. A geological hammer up to 0.5 kg (16 oz) is recommended. The chisel should be strong enough to use with stone or it may wear out quickly. Take great care with these tools. Thick, protective gloves are recommended, plus eye protection to shield your eyes from any shards of rock that may fly up.

Wrapping
For fragile specimens, use paper towels or soft foam wrapping with rubber bands to secure your fossils for the journey home.

Brush
Useful onsite and at home, a soft-bristled brush will help you remove grit and dust from your fossil so you can enjoy its finest details.

OTHER USEFUL THINGS

Take notes
Carry a notebook and pen to record where and when you located your finds. Take photos, too. You could also add sketches of your fossils and names once you have identified them.

Magnifying glass
A fold-out magnifying glass can be useful for examining fine detail on rocks during your search and at home.

Fossil displays

If you are able to take fossils home, you'll want to clean them, study them closely, and prepare your collection for display. If you took only photos, print, label, and display them as you would a physical specimen.

Dust and grime
Start by gently removing any sand or earth from each stone using a soft brush. An old toothbrush or soft, clean paintbrush is good for this. A pair of tweezers or metal dental probes can be used for removing any cemented stone covering your fossil. Work slowly and carefully to avoid damaging the fossil itself.

Display box
Store your fossils in open trays. Include a label with the details of each fossil—what it is, plus where and when you found it, and the geological age of the rock, if known. Keep a matching record of your finds in a notebook or on a computer file.

Further study

As you find more fossils, you may want to take your hobby further. Local fossil or geological groups can help you identify finds and are happy to accept new members interested in geology and paleontology. Groups also arrange regular lectures and field trips. Visits to natural history museums offer the opportunity to look at the rarest of fossils, including those of dinosaurs and other prehistoric reptiles.

Identifying your fossils

What do you have in your hands? How many millions of years old is it? Finding out the name and age of your fossils is part of the fun.

The name game

Fossils have scientific names, just as living plants and animals do. The first part of the name is the genus, the second part the species. So, for *Tyrannosaurus rex*, *Tyrannosaurus* is the genus, *rex* is the species. The name means "king of the tyrant lizards" (although it was a reptile, it was not a lizard).

Many species are named for what makes them unique, for where they are found, or after people. The fossil *Auroralumina attenboroughii* is a 560-million-year-old fossilized sea creature named after the broadcaster and natural historian Sir David Attenborough. Some fossils are named after characters in *The Lord of the Rings* and the Harry Potter books!

Top 10 fossils

The first, the most historically important, and the most expensive—here are the top 10 greatest fossil finds. Best of luck unearthing one of these treasures!

1 Apex Chert

What may be the world's oldest fossils were found in fine-grained sedimentary rock known as Apex Chert in Australia. The microscopic remains—0.5 to 20 micrometers across—date from about 3.5 billion years ago. They are believed to be single-celled blue-green algae called cyanobacteria, though some experts suggest they are the remains of minerals.

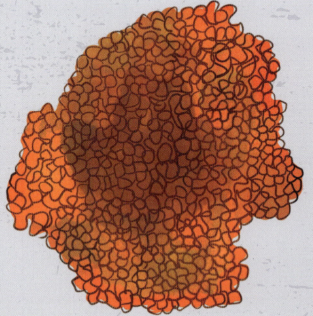

2 Eukaryotes

This fossil of algae-like growth found in China is proof of complex multicellular life dating from 1,800 million years ago, in the Proterozoic. Scientists have since provided evidence that these eukaryotes (living organisms made up of cells with a nucleus) have been around for 2,230 million years.

③ Montsechia vidalii

The oldest example of a flowering plant, this fossil, unearthed from limestone in Spanish mountains, grew in Early Cretaceous swamps 130 million years ago.

④ Metaspriggina

Dating from 505 million years ago, in the Cambrian Period, this Canadian fossil is the earliest evidence of a fish with details of eyes, nostrils, and jaws preserved in the rock.

⑤ Megalosaurus femur

When this Jurassic fossil was dug up in England in 1676, it was thought to be a thigh bone belonging to an elephant or giant human. It was another 150 years before geologist William Buckland gave it the name *Megalosaurus*, meaning "great lizard."

Dinosaur ID

In 1842, this *Megalosaurus* fossil was one of the three fossils that Richard Owen used to classify the very first dinosaurs.

Archaeopteryx

Discovered in Germany in 1861, this limestone fossil was the first to link dinosaurs and birds. With teeth, claws, a bony tail, plus feathered wings, this 147-million-year-old animal from the Late Jurassic Period is considered the earliest bird.

Ichthyosaur

Mary Anning was an amateur fossil hunter who scoured the south coast of Britain for treasure in the early nineteenth century. She found this skeleton of a marine predator in the cliffs, the remains of what would later be named *Ichthyosaur* ("fish lizard") and dated to the Early Jurassic Period, around 200 million years ago. The site of her discovery is now a hugely popular haunt for fossil hunters.

Diplodocus

Probably the world's most famous fossil, the original was discovered in Wyoming, USA, in 1899. It lived in the Late Jurassic Period, approximately 150 million years ago, and is displayed in the Carnegie Museum of Natural History in Pittsburgh, USA.

 A BIG welcome

Known as Dippy, this 26 m (85 ft) cast of a *Diplodocus carnegii* fossil filled the entrance hall of London's Natural History Museum from 1979 to 2017.

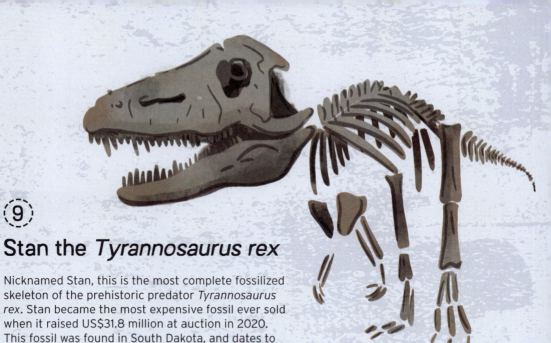

⑨ Stan the *Tyrannosaurus rex*

Nicknamed Stan, this is the most complete fossilized skeleton of the prehistoric predator *Tyrannosaurus rex*. Stan became the most expensive fossil ever sold when it raised US$31.8 million at auction in 2020. This fossil was found in South Dakota, and dates to around 66 million years ago, in the Cretaceous Period. Stan will be the star attraction at the new Abu Dhabi Natural History Museum in the United Arab Emirates.

⑩ Lucy

This incomplete fossilized skeleton of an *Australopithecus afarensis* female was discovered in Ethiopia in 1974. An early human ancestor, this 1.1 m (3 ft 7 in) female, nicknamed Lucy after a song by the Beatles, dates from about 3.2 million years ago.

CHAPTER 2: PLANTS

Plants are living organisms that use sunlight to make food. The fossil history of plants shows them developing over millions of years from simple marine algae to plants that could colonize dry land, with roots, stems, leaves, then flowers, while wooden fibers allowed them to rise toward the light as trees.

Algae

Algae are the earliest type of plant to appear on Earth. They may have first appeared in the oceans over a billion years ago. Types of algae range from single-celled organisms to multicellular plants like today's seaweeds.

Receptaculites oweni

ORDER: Dasycladales
FAMILY: Receptaculitaceae
PERIOD: Cambrian–Permian, 488–250 million years ago
SIZE: Up to 30 cm (12 in) diameter
RARITY: Rare

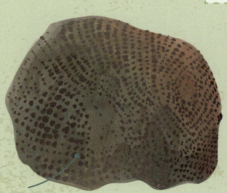

Once thought to be the remains of a coral or sponge, the *Receptaculites* is commonly known as a sunflower coral but is not a coral and certainly not a flower. The spiral pattern is thought to be created by simple plants called dasycladacean algae.

The diamond shapes over the fossil's surface are the tops of shafts called meroms that grew from the alga's center.

Algae do not have true roots, leaves, flowers, or fruit containing seeds. Nor do they have woody parts that can raise them out of water. Algae reproduce by releasing spores. Like land plants, algae use photosynthesis to make energy from sunlight. In the process they convert carbon dioxide into oxygen, which most living things need to survive.

THE LIVING ORGANISM: *RECEPTACULITES*

Believed to be a form of algae, *Receptaculites* attached to rocks and grew into round structures up to 30 cm (12 in) across. They helped build reefs during the Ordovician Period, around 485 to 443 million years ago.

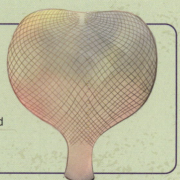

Cooksonia pertoni

ORDER: Rhyniales
FAMILY: Rhyniaceae
PERIOD: Late Silurian–Mid Devonian, 433–393 million years ago
SIZE: 5 cm (2 in) height
RARITY: Rare

Early land plants

About 500 million years ago, plants made their way onto land. The arrival of plants helped add oxygen to the air and provided a food source for animals, which would follow plant life out of the water.

Cooksonia was a simple plant with branching stems but no leaves or roots.

To avoid drying up under the sun, *Cooksonia* transported water, along with nutrients from soil, through a vascular system in its stems.

The trumpet-like tops of each stem are called sporangia. These helped the plant reproduce by releasing spores, like modern-day fungi.

THE LIVING ORGANISM: *COOKSONIA*
This plant used photosynthesis to make food from sunlight and was probably green. While only rising just above the ground, the plant successfully spread worldwide.

Chalk cliffs

The famous white cliffs of Dover on the south coast of England are made up of chalk from the Cretaceous Period. The chalk is the limestone skeletal remains of microscopic single-celled algae called coccolithophorids.

Liverworts

Liverworts are low-growing plants with flat, fleshy bodies. They do not have roots or a vascular system. Instead, water is absorbed directly through the plant's surface.

Metzgeriothallus sharonae

ORDER: Marchantiales
FAMILY: Marchantiaceae
PERIOD: Mid Devonian-present day, 390 million years ago-
SIZE: Up to 2 cm (0.8 in) height
RARITY: Rare

Liverworts lack stems, leaves, and roots but they sprout rhizoids—root-like growths that keep them anchored.

The main part of the plant is called the thallus, which takes in moisture from the water and air.

Liverwort fossils are rare, as their soft, fleshy parts do not survive for long.

THE MODERN WORLD
Thousands of species of liverwort can be found today, growing in damp, shady places. These mossy plants got their name because their fleshy shape was thought to resemble animal livers. The umbrella-like growths hold the female reproductive parts.

26

Horsetails

Forests spread overland through the Carboniferous Period, with tall, tree-like *Calamites* among them. *Calamites* were members of the horsetail family, a plant with a hollow central trunk and upward sprouting leaves.

Annularia stellata

ORDER: Equisetales
FAMILY: Calamitaceae
PERIOD: Carboniferous–Early Permian, 360–250 million years ago
SIZE: Up to 30 m (100 ft) height
RARITY: Uncommon

The fossilized foliage of *Calamites* is called *Annularia*. The soft, pointed leaves grew at regular intervals, spreading open like umbrellas.

Calamites reproduced by releasing microscopic spores from cones, and through an underground network of rhizomes, as ferns do today.

Impressions of *Annularia* are often been found in coal. Coal is the remains of prehistoric plants that grew mostly during the Carboniferous Period.

THE LIVING ORGANISM: *CALAMITES*
Forests of *Calamites* grew near water during the Carboniferous and Permian Period. These ancient horsetails resembled trees and could tower up to 30 m (100 ft) tall with 60 cm (24 in)-diameter bamboo-like trunks made of xylem.

 ## Forest scrub

Species of horsetail are still found today, sprouting from swampy conditions. The plants are also known as "scouring rushes," as the rough stems were once used as scouring pads for cleaning dishes.

True ferns

The first ferns appeared in the Mid-Devonian Period. They were hugely successful plants without seeds or flowers that became common throughout the Carboniferous Period.

Psaronius

ORDER: Marattiales
FAMILY: Psaroniaceae
PERIOD: Mid-Devonian–present day, 390 million years ago–
SIZE: Up to 10 m (33 ft) height
RARITY: Common

Psaronius was the name initially given to the fossilized stem of this plant only, with the preserved fronds given the name *Pecopteris*. These were later discovered to be from the same plant.

Tree ferns are not strictly trees as their trunks are not made from true wood but from a leaf base that is thickened near the ground by small roots.

True ferns reproduce by releasing spores from capsules called sporangia on the underside of their fronds.

THE LIVING ORGANISM: *PSARONIUS*

Psaronius was a tree fern that towered up to 10 m (33 ft) in height, with 3 m (10 ft)-long fronds sprouting from the top of its trunk. Ferns grow best in moist conditions and even shade. Their fossils are mostly found in coal deposits from prehistoric swamps.

Seed ferns

The plants commonly known as seed ferns had similar foliage but differed from true ferns by reproducing using seeds rather than spores.

Neuropteris lancifera

ORDER: Medullosales
FAMILY: Medullosaceae
PERIOD: Late Carboniferous–Early Permian, 325–270 million years ago
SIZE: Up to 10 m (33 ft) height
RARITY: Uncommon

The leaflets, or pinnae, that sprout along the stalk are rounded rather than toothed.

Some *Medullosa* leaf fossils show evidence of being nibbled by insects.

Fronds are the most commonly found fossilized remains of the seed-bearing plant *Medullosa*.

SETTING SEED
Fossilized casts of *Medullosa* seed pods have been unearthed. They resemble large nuts, the size of an avocado, with three ribs. The fossilized pods have their own name, *Trigonocarpus*. They produced pollen that may have been distributed by insects.

THE LIVING ORGANISM: *MEDULLOSA*
The seed fern *Medullosa* grew mostly in swamps and beside rivers. It looked very much like a tree fern, with a trunk made from old leaf bases and with anchoring roots sprouting near the ground. It had large egg-sized seeds which hung from its stems.

Scale trees

A common plant found in swamps during the Carboniferous Period, scale trees could reach enormous heights. Fossils of scale tree bark are often found in coal deposits.

Lepidodendron bretonense

ORDER: Lepidodendrales
FAMILY: Lepidodendraceae
PERIOD: Carboniferous, 359–299 million years ago
SIZE: Up to 50 m (160 ft) height
RARITY: Very common

The diamond pattern on the bark is made from the scars of fallen stems and leaves.

The plant's narrow, needle-like leaves grew in a spiral pattern around the trunk.

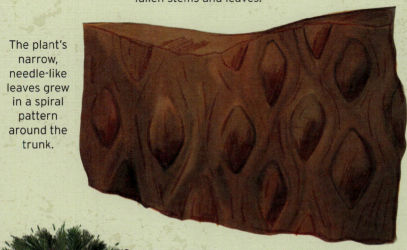

Cigar-shaped cones, *Lepidostrobus*, containing spores, grew from the tips of leaves.

The scale tree *Lepidodendron* was one of the largest trees of its time.

THE LIVING ORGANISM: SCALE TREES
Scale trees thrived in damp conditions. They were among the first plants with roots to grow into trees many meters tall. The trunks could be as wide as 2 m (6.6 ft) at their base, tapering at the top. Most scale trees grew fast as they only lived for 10 to 15 years.

Fossil fuel

Coal, burned as a fossil fuel today, is a mineral formed over millions of years from the remains of Carboniferous Period plants such as scale trees, ferns, and horsetails. The plants were buried in swamps, before huge pressures and temperatures below the Earth's surface carbonized the plant matter. The resulting coal is mined from underground seams.

Bennettitales

Closely resembling cycads, with thick trunks and frond-like leaves, *Bennettitales* thrived from the Triassic to the Cretaceous Period, when they became extinct.

Williamsonia gigas

ORDER: Bennettitales
FAMILY: Williamsoniaceae
PERIOD: Mid Triassic–Cretaceous, 230–66 million years ago
SIZE: Up to 3 m (10 ft) height
RARITY: Rare

This ironstone fossil preserves part of the flower-like reproductive part of *Williamsonia*.

The preserved plant parts are bracts, the woody protection for the seed-bearing flower-like part inside.

Williamsonia may be the ancestor of later flowering plants.

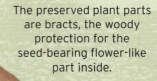

THE LIVING ORGANISM: BENNETTITALES

The tough, diamond-patterned trunk of *Bennettitales* was made from the bases of old leaves and resembled a stretched, woody pineapple. The frond-like foliage sprouted from the top and branches.

Conifers

Conifers are a group of forest-growing trees that includes firs, spruce, cedars, yews, and the world's tallest living tree, the sequoia.

Metasequoia glyptostroboides

ORDER: Cupressales
FAMILY: Cupressaceae
PERIOD: Cretaceous–present day, 100 million years ago–
SIZE: Up to 50 m (165 ft) height
RARITY: Uncommon

Pine cones are commonly found as fossils in the Late Cretaceous rocks of Hell Creek, South Dakota, USA.

Conifers are cone-bearing trees and shrubs. Both male and female woody cones are grown. The male cone releases pollen that is caught by sticky sap in the female cone, where it fertilizes the seeds.

This fossil is of *Metasequoia*, a type of redwood with small, rounded cones, and leaves that sprout in opposing pairs from the main shoot.

Conifer leaves are usually needle-like and glossy to retain moisture.

Pine cones are the tough seed-bearing parts of conifers. Examples like this rounded cone from *Metasequoia* are typically about 2 cm (0.75 in) across.

The splits in the cone are where the seeds were stored before release.

TRIASSIC TO TODAY
The ginkgo or maidenhair tree has been growing on Earth since the Late Triassic Period. It is a seed-bearing tree, like conifers but deciduous, with fan-shaped broad leaves. As with *Metasequoia*, it has survived since prehistoric times in parts of eastern Asia, before being discovered by Western botanists and exported worldwide from the late seventeenth century.

THE MODERN WORLD
Conifers dominated the dry uplands during the Triassic and Jurassic Periods. Fossilized *Metasequoia*, from the later Cretaceous Period, was first named in 1941 and considered extinct but, just months later, living examples were discovered in a valley in Sichuan Province, China. These water fir trees were finally identified as *Metasequoia*, or Dawn Redwood, in 1946.

Flowering plants

Flowering plants first appeared during the Early Cretaceous Period. They now make up the vast majority of plants on Earth.

Magnolia boulayana

ORDER: Magnoliales
FAMILY: Magnoliaceae
PERIOD: Cretaceous–present day, 95 million years ago–
SIZE: Up to 40 m (130 ft) height
RARITY: Common

Magnolia grew before the evolution of bees, so it was probably first pollinated by beetles.

The leaves are wide and flat, with a main vein from stalk to leaf tip and thinner, lateral veins leading from it.

Because they are fragile, there are few fossils of flowers from flowering plants, but many of their leaves.

This fossilized imprint of a leaf belongs to magnolia, a flowering plant that has survived to the modern day and is appreciated for its large blooms.

THE ANCIENT WORLD

The earliest flowers did not have obvious petals. They were simple and very small, but structured like flowers today. Flowers became showier by the Late Cretaceous, with plants like magnolia. These attracted beetles as pollinators. The use of insects to transfer pollen from flower to flower is a more efficient way of reproducing than relying on wind or water.

QUICK RECOVERY

Flowering plants had important advantages over conifers. They could reproduce quickly, sometimes growing and producing seeds in a single year. This was hugely useful when dinosaurs such as hadrosaurs developed the ability to chew vegetable matter and graze on leafy plants. Not only could the flowering plants recover quickly, but they also evolved new ways to spread their seeds—in dinosaur dung!

Montsechia vidalii

ORDER: Ceratophyllales
FAMILY: Montsechiaceae
PERIOD: Early Cretaceous, 130–125 million years ago
SIZE: Several meters in length
RARITY: Rare

FIRST BLOOM

This fossil of the aquatic plant *Montsechia vidalii* may be evidence of the first flowering plant on Earth. The impression of a water weed was found in the Spanish Pyrenees more than a century ago but only recently recognized as being 130 million years old, from the Early Cretaceous.

Fossilized wood

Petrified forests around the world contain the remains of prehistoric trees, where the wood has turned to stone. The remains are often left on display on the ground.

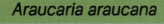

Araucaria araucana

ORDER: Araucariales
FAMILY: Araucariaceae
PERIOD: Triassic–present day, 230 million years ago–
SIZE: Up to 40 m (130 ft) height
RARITY: Common

The wood has been replaced with silica, giving the fossil an attractive colored pattern.

Cones from *Araucaria* trees have also survived as fossils.

This petrified wood from Madagascar is a slice of the trunk from a 220-million-year-old *Araucaria* tree.

PETRIFICATION
For whole tree trunks to be petrified, the wood had to be buried by water or volcanic ash and compressed underground for millions of years. Over this time, groundwater seeped into the wood, with the water's minerals (silica or calcium carbonate) slowly replacing the organic material.

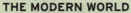

THE MODERN WORLD
Araucaria araucana, also known as the pewen or monkey puzzle tree, is an evergreen conifer native to South America. This and other species of *Araucaria* date back to the Triassic Period, when they were found worldwide. The cone-bearing trees had one main stem that grew to a height of 40 m (130 ft), in reach of sauropod dinosaurs (page 82). The leaves were needle-like or triangular and spiky, and arranged in a spiral pattern around the stem.

Amber

Amber is the fossilized resin produced by trees, mostly conifers from the Carboniferous Period. On rare occasions, this resin would trap and preserve insects, lizards, or plant matter.

Amber

PERIOD: Cretaceous
145 million years ago
RARITY: Rare

This resin from a prehistoric pine tree has captured a mosquito, preserving it in all its detail.

Traces of iron found in preserved mosquitoes is evidence that they fed on blood.

Prehistoric mosquitoes are very similar to species living today.

Amber has been treasured for millennia and set into jewelry.

THE LIVING ORGANISM: INSECTS

Insects appeared on Earth in the Devonian Period. These small, wingless creatures evolved into the first flying creatures by the Carboniferous Period. Mosquitoes have been around for more than 100 million years and would once have fed on bird, mammal, and possibly dinosaur blood.

Dino DNA

The first *Jurassic Park* movie showed scientists retrieving dinosaur DNA from a prehistoric insect trapped in amber. Despite the excellent preservation of insects with hair and wings in fossilized resin, no DNA survives.

CHAPTER 3: INVERTEBRATES

Invertebrates, animals without backbones, first appear in the fossil record about 575 million years ago as simple animals lacking organs, even brains. Invertebrates include marine species such as jellyfish and octopuses, the commonly found fossil species trilobites and ammonites, plus insects and spiders.

Early invertebrates

The earliest animal fossils are hard to interpret, as they are so different from life that we recognize. Complex multicellular life forms evolved in the oceans. Without predators, these creatures did not need armor. Their bodies were soft.

Dickinsonia costata

ORDER: Uncertain
FAMILY: Dickinsoniidae
PERIOD: Late Precambrian, 570–541 million years ago
SIZE: Up to 1.4 m (4.6 ft) in length
RARITY: Rare

Which end is which? It is not known which is the front and which the back for this mysterious Precambrian creature named *Dickinsonia*.

Despite many fossil casts and imprints being unearthed from sandstone, little detail of internal organs has been found.

THE LIVING ORGANISM: *DICKINSONIA*
Although considered one of the world's earliest animals, little is known about *Dickinsonia*. Was it a jellyfish? A segmented flat worm? *Dickinsonia* lived on the sea bed about 570 million years ago and varied in size from 4 mm (0.2 in) to about 1.4 m (4.6 ft) long. Whether it moved on its own or was pushed along by currents is unknown.

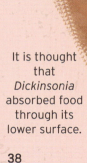

It is thought that *Dickinsonia* absorbed food through its lower surface.

Sponges

Sponges are simple animals that attach themselves to rocks and mud on the sea bed. They lack organs, muscles, or a nervous system, and feed by filtering passing food particles through their porous bodies.

Raphidonema farringdonense

ORDER: Stellispongiida
FAMILY: Endostomatidae
PERIOD: Cretaceous–Paleogene, 136–37 million years ago
SIZE: 8 cm (3.2 in) height
RARITY: Common

Sponge remains are common enough to be used as index fossils and date the strata they are found in.

Raphidonema is found in abundance in the Farringdon Sponge Gravels of Oxfordshire, England, where millions of years ago it formed sponge-beds, like reefs.

Different sponge species may grow branches or form chimney or fungi-like structures. *Raphidonema* is shaped like a lumpy funnel, with a smooth interior.

THE LIVING ORGANISM: *RAPHIDONEMA*

Raphidonema was a common sponge that grew in shallow, warm waters during the Cretaceous Period. Its body formed a funnel shape. Sponge cells are independent of one another. If a sponge is passed through a sieve, the cells can regrow into a new sponge.

Corals

Corals are part of the same group as jellyfish and urchins. While few soft-bodied jellyfish and urchins are preserved as fossils, the limestone skeletons of corals are more hardy and have survived burial on the sea bed and fossilization.

Halysites labyrinthicus

ORDER: Favositida
FAMILY: Halysitidae
PERIOD: Late Ordovician–Early Devonian, 461–416 million years ago
SIZE: Up to 20 cm (8 in) across
RARITY: Common

There are three main types of coral found as fossils—horn corals (rugosa), tabulate corals (tabulate), and stony corals (scleractinia).

This coral colony is *Halysites*, tabulate corals also known as chain corals because the tube walls (corallites) form beaded patterns that look like chains from above.

THE LIVING ORGANISM: *HALYSITES*

Corals begin life as tiny, tentacled creatures called polyps. These quickly settle on a hard surface on the sea bed and build an outer mineral skeleton. Over time, colonies of polyps can build giant coral structures called reefs. *Halysites* appeared as a tight arrangement of tubes. Each tube would have contained a feeding polyp near the top.

WIPE OUT

Rugose and tabulate corals were lost in a series of extinctions at the end of the Permian Period, 252 million years ago. Over 90 percent of invertebrates were wiped out during this period. This was possibly due to the forming of a supercontinent called Pangaea, which caused the loss of environments for these corals and a change in sea levels. By the middle of the Triassic Period, new corals began to appear. These scleractinian corals took the place of the lost species and are the ancestors of modern-day corals.

Bryozoans

Resembling small corals, bryozoans are colonies of simple tentacled marine creatures called zooids that sift seawater for food.

Fenestella antiqua

ORDER: Fenestrida
FAMILY: Fenestellidae
PERIOD: Ordovician–Triassic, 480–230 million years ago
SIZE: 5 cm (2 in) height
RARITY: Rare

This fossil is of the lace coral *Fenestella*. The many upright branches are connected by crossbars called dissepiments.

This bryozoan was found in rocks from the Silurian to the Permian Period.

Complete fossils of bryozoan colonies are very rare, but broken pieces may be found in shale and limestone.

THE LIVING ORGANISM: *FENESTELLA*

Fenestella, also known as lace coral, formed a cone-shaped net around 5 cm (2 in) tall. It fed on food particles that passed one way through its holes. While this species became extinct, about 3,500 species of bryozoans survive today.

Graptolites

Graptolites were small, floating colonies of marine creatures. Some formed leaflike shapes, others ribbons. Their fossilized remains can be mistaken for plants.

Oktavites spiralis

ORDER: Graptoloidea
FAMILY: Monograptidae
PERIOD: Silurian–Early Devonian, 435–410 million years ago
SIZE: Up to 20 cm (4.75 in) diameter
RARITY: Common

The name graptolite comes from the Greek for "writing in the rocks," as this is how the fossilized remains were interpreted thousands of years ago.

Graptolites can be mistaken for plants because they left imprints that may resemble leaves or fronds.

Graptolites are most often preserved as impressions in shale. Their evolutionary speed and abundance makes them useful as index fossils.

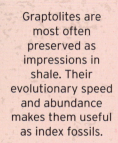

THE LIVING ORGANISM: GRAPTOLITES

Graptolites took many forms, from pencil shapes to spiky corkscrews like *Monograptus spiralis*. Graptolites became extinct during the Carboniferous Period, possibly because these floating colonies of simple animals would have proved easy prey for jawed fish (page 66).

Worms

Prehistoric soft-bodied, segmented worms are rarely preserved, but the tubes they lived inside may survive as fossils.

Rotularia bognoriensis

ORDER: Canalipalpata
FAMILY: Serpulidae
PERIOD: Jurassic–Paleogene, 150–34 million years ago
SIZE: 2 cm (0.7 in) diameter
RARITY: Common

Several casts of the marine worm *Rotularia* have been preserved in this fossil.

Fossils of *Rotularia* were first thought to be evidence of sea snails due to their coiled appearance.

The spirals are the remains of a calcite tube secreted by the worm as its protective home.

THE LIVING ORGANISM: *ROTULARIA*
Rotularia was a worm that made its home in a tight spiral tube. After an early period of life attached to the sea bed, *Rotularia* lived freely, exploring shallow seas for food.

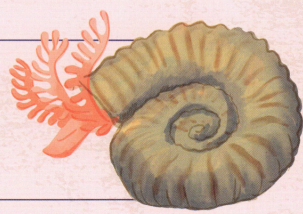

Trilobites

Trilobites were arthropods, related to insects, arachnids, and crustaceans. These hugely successful and varied sea creatures thrived on Earth for more than 250 million years.

Elrathia kingii

ORDER: Ptychopariida
FAMILY: Ptychopariacea
PERIOD: Cambrian, 513–498 million years ago
SIZE: Up to 5 cm (2 in) in length
RARITY: Very common

Trilobite shells are the most common fossils to be found from the Cambrian Period. Fossils of the creature's softer parts—legs, gills, antennae—are rare.

Trilobite means "three-lobed" for the divisions in its body from left to right. Like insects, trilobites also had three parts to their bodies from top to bottom—a head, thorax, and tail.

Elrathia is a thumb-sized trilobite, a common find in North American fossil sites.

THE LIVING ORGANISM: TRILOBITES
Trilobites were beetle-like arthropods with armored shells that crawled over the sea bed in search of food. Some swam, and some even ventured onto land.

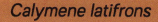

Calymene latifrons

ORDER: Phacopida
FAMILY: Phacopidae
PERIOD: Late Ordovician–Late Devonian, 457–360 million years ago
SIZE: Up to 15 cm (6 in) in length
RARITY: Rare

Phacops has a pronounced knobbly forehead, known as a glabella, between its eyes.

Most trilobites had compound eyes, like flies, but a few were eyeless.

If threatened, trilobites could curl up like a hedgehog, as this fossilized *Phacops* shows. Some trilobites even had spines on their shells for extra protection.

All arthropods have shells (exoskeletons), which they shed as they grow.

GIANT SIZE
Trilobites ranged in size from peppercorn-sized to giants. *Acanthopleurella stipulae* was just 1.5 mm (0.06 in) long, while *Isotelus rex* grew to 72 cm (28 in) in length.

Crustaceans

Fossilized crustaceans are mostly marine creatures with exoskeletons like modern-day crabs, shrimp, and lobsters.

Eryma mandelslohi

ORDER: Decapoda
FAMILY: Erymidae
PERIOD: Jurassic–Late Cretaceous, 200–70 million years ago
SIZE: 6 cm (2.5 in) in length
RARITY: Rare

Ten-legged decapods, such as prawns, first appeared in the Ordovician Period. These were followed by shrimp and crabs in the Jurassic and Cretaceous Periods.

This fossil of *Eryma*, the first known true lobster, was found in German limestone in an area that was once the shore of the prehistoric Tethys Sea.

THE LIVING ORGANISM: *ERYMA*
Eryma was only about 6 cm (2.5 in) long, but otherwise resembled a modern-day lobster, with two front pincers used for capturing food and defense, and a segmented abdomen and tail fan used for propulsion.

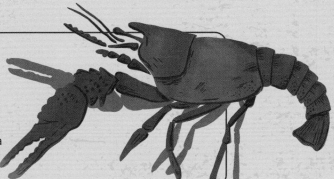

Paleocarpilius macrocheilus

ORDER: Decapoda
FAMILY: Carpiliidae
PERIOD: Paleogene, 49–28 million years ago
SIZE: 9 cm (3.5 in) diameter
RARITY: Common

The right pincer is noticeably larger than the left, a feature of some modern-day crabs and lobsters.

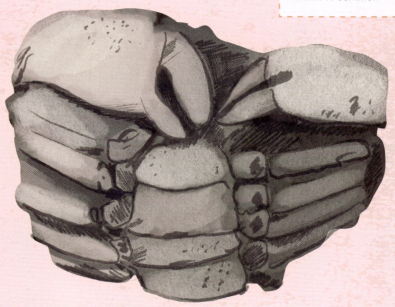

Palaeocarpilius is an extinct mud crab found as a fossil in Europe and Africa.

The crab reached a size of 9 cm (3.5 in) in diameter. Complete specimens are rare, but separated claws are commonly found.

TUNNEL TRACES
While fossils of tiny shrimp are rare, trace fossils that record their movements can be found. *Thalassinoides* and *Ophiomorpha* are the names given to fossilized casts of a tunnel network left by shrimp from the Jurassic and Late Cretaceous Periods. The bumpy texture of the tunnel walls was caused by the shrimps adding balls of mud to burrow walls.

Brachiopods

Brachiopods are marine creatures that feed on the sea bed. They live in a shell made of two halves, or valves, often hinged. While there are only about 120 types living today, more than 4,500 brachiopod genera have been discovered.

Platystrophia ponderosa

ORDER: Orthida
FAMILY: Plectorthidae
PERIOD: Ordovician–Silurian, 468–419 million years ago
SIZE: 4 cm (1.5 in) in length
RARITY: Very common

Brachiopod fossils are fairly common. When they die, their shell shuts tight, so most fossils are complete specimens.

Platystrophia is a hinged or articulate brachiopod. Brachiopods with non-hinged shells are called inarticulate.

Brachiopods, with one slightly larger shell, are commonly known as lamp shells as they resemble an antique oil lamp.

THE LIVING ORGANISM: BRACHIOPODS

Most brachiopods attach themselves to the sea floor with a stalk called a pedicle that emerges near the hinge between the shells. They filter for food by opening and closing their shell. Brachiopods do not have eyes but sense changes around them through bristles just inside their shell. Prehistoric brachiopods ranged in size from those as small as a pinhead to the 30 cm (12 in)-wide *Gigantoproductus*.

Butterfly shells

Mucrospirifer is a brachiopod from the Devonian Period with a winglike shape, which has led to it being nicknamed butterfly shell. In ancient China, it was known as a stone swallow and thought to have magical properties.

Crinoids

Crinoids are sometimes mistaken for plants, with their feathery fronds and stalk rooted on the sea bed, but they are actually echinoderms, animals related to sea urchins and sea stars.

Dimerocrinites decadactylus

ORDER: Diplobathrida
FAMILY: Dimerocrinitidae
PERIOD: Silurian–Early Devonian, 439–419 million years ago
SIZE: Up to 1 m (3.3 ft) in length
RARITY: Rare

Crinoids were abundant in the Paleozoic Era. Many species were likely to have been an important food source for predators.

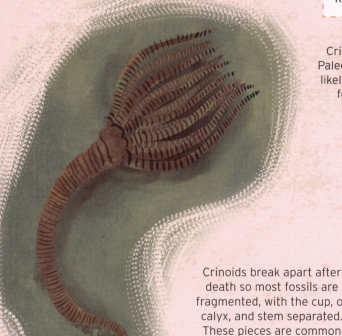

Crinoids break apart after death so most fossils are fragmented, with the cup, or calyx, and stem separated. These pieces are common fossils. Complete examples of crinoids, like this *Dimerocrinites*, are very rare.

THE LIVING ORGANISM: CRINOIDS

Crinoids are also known as sea lilies for their plant-like appearance. These animals could crawl across the sea bed but tended to plant their flexible stalk in one position in the sand. They filtered food from the water using feathery branches sprouting from the cup-like main body, which contained its organs, mouth, and stomach. A few species, mostly stemless feather stars, survived the extinction of most crinoids at the end of the Permian Period.

Different species of crinoid are identified by the pattern of plates around their cup (calyx) and around their stalk.

FAIRY MONEY
Star-shaped fossilized slices of stems from the crinoid *Pentacrinites* are sometimes called fairy money or star stones.

Bivalves

Bivalves are mollusks, the group of creatures that includes snails and octopuses, with two matching hinged shells or valves.

Pecten Tenuis

ORDER: Ptychopariida
FAMILY: Ptychopariacea
PERIOD: Cambrian, 513–498 million years ago
SIZE: Up to 5 cm (2 in) in length
RARITY: Very common

This bivalve with a ribbed, fan-shaped shell is called *Pecten*, a relative of today's scallop.

The edges of paired bivalve shells often interlock with each other.

Prehistoric *Pecten* dated from the Mid-Ordovician Period and some species grew to about 8 cm (3 in) across.

THE LIVING ORGANISM: *PECTEN*
Bivalves are filter feeders and often bury themselves in sediment on the sea bed, which has led to many being preserved as fossils. *Pecten*, like modern-day scallops, had a strong adductor muscle that allowed it to open and close its shell and propel itself through the water to escape predators. Common bivalves today include oysters, mussels, and clams.

Trigonia interlaevigata

ORDER: Trigoniida
FAMILY: Trigoniidae
PERIOD: Permian–Paleogene, 298–56 million years ago
SIZE: Up to 10 cm (4 in) in length
RARITY: Very common

The saltwater bivalve *Trigonia*, from the Triassic Period, was thought to have become extinct 65 million years ago until a living example, *Neotrigonia,* was discovered in Australia in 1802.

The grooves on *Trigonia*'s shell would have helped it burrow into the sandy sea bed.

The name *Trigonia* means "triangular" in Greek.

TOE CURLING

The curled appearance of *Gryphaea*, the fossilized remains of a bivalve mollusk, led to it gaining the name devil's toenails. These common fossils from the Triassic and Jurassic Periods were once collected and used as ingredients in folk medicine.

Gastropods

Gastropods have survived in various forms for 530 million years, with over 60,000 species living today, in the sea, fresh water, and on land.

Turritella robusta

ORDER: Sorbeoconcha
FAMILY: Turritellidae
PERIOD: Late Jurassic–present day, 237 million years ago–
SIZE: Up to 20 cm (8 in) in length
RARITY: Common

The soft body parts of gastropods tend not to survive fossilization, but the shells are commonly found.

Gastropod shells are generally spiral in form and made of the mineral aragonite or calcite. Some are wound into dome shapes. Others, like these fossilized *Turritella* shells, form long cones.

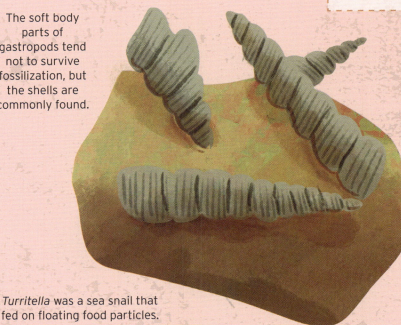

Turritella was a sea snail that fed on floating food particles.

THE LIVING ORGANISM: GASTROPODS
Gastropods are mollusks that mostly live in shells. They have a head, with eyes and a mouth plus a large flat foot for slithering over surfaces. Some dig into sediment on search of food. Between the Cambrian and Devonian Periods all gastropods lived in the oceans. They began to move into freshwater and crawl onto land during the Carboniferous Period.

Platyceras pulcherrimum

ORDER: Archaeogastropoda
FAMILY: Platyceratidae
PERIOD: Silurian–Mid Triassic, 439–221 million years ago
SIZE: 2 cm (0.75 in) in length
RARITY: Very common

Platyceras was a sea snail that lived from the Silurian to the Triassic Period.

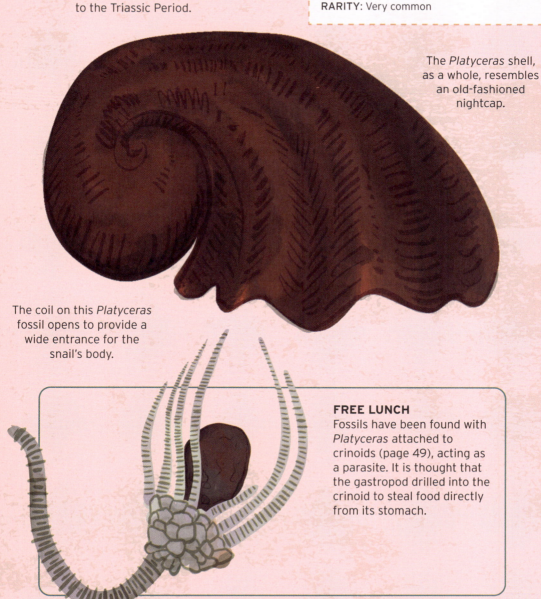

The *Platyceras* shell, as a whole, resembles an old-fashioned nightcap.

The coil on this *Platyceras* fossil opens to provide a wide entrance for the snail's body.

FREE LUNCH
Fossils have been found with *Platyceras* attached to crinoids (page 49), acting as a parasite. It is thought that the gastropod drilled into the crinoid to steal food directly from its stomach.

Belemnites

Belemnites were close relatives of squid and cuttlefish. Their bullet-shaped tail guards are commonly found as fossils.

Cylindroteuthis puzosiana

ORDER: Belemnitida
FAMILY: Cylindroteuthididae
PERIOD: Jurassic, 165–145 million years ago
SIZE: 25 cm (10 in) in length
RARITY: Common

The calcite tail guard of belemnites, called the rostrum, is often found as a fossil, sometimes in groups called a belemnite battleground.

The rostrum may have worked as a counterbalance for the swimming belemnite.

Preserved rostra are found in a variety of shapes, including wide cigar forms, and several pinched at the tip. This Jurassic *Cylindroteuthis* fossil, from a species that grew up to 25 cm (10 in) in length, is thin like a javelin.

THE LIVING ORGANISM: BELEMNITES
Like squid, belemnites were cephalopods, with a long, soft body and internal skeleton. They are thought to have had 10 hooked tentacles surrounding their beak-like mouth (radula), fins on the tail, and an ink sac like living squid. Most belemnites were about finger-length but one, *Megateuthis gigantea*, may have grown to 70 cm (28 in) in length. They were a food source for marine predators such as plesiosaurs (page 78), ichthyosaurs (page 77), and crocodilians (page 74).

DARTS FROM HEAVEN
One early explanation for belemnites was that they were darts from heaven, fired toward Earth during thunderstorms. In Germany, they received the names devil's fingers and ghostly candles.

Nautiloids

Nautiloids are the only cephalopods with an external shell that still survive today in a few species, including the pearly nautilus. In prehistoric times, nautiloids were numerous and for a while included the largest creatures in the oceans.

Orthoceras regulare

ORDER: Orthocerida
FAMILY: Orthoceratidae
PERIOD: Mid Ordovician, 470–458 million years ago
SIZE: 15 cm (6 in) in length
RARITY: Very common

The nautiloid's shell contained several chambers that the nautiloid could fill with gas to control buoyancy. The shell would have floated horizontally.

The chambered part of the nautiloid's shell is called the phragmocone.

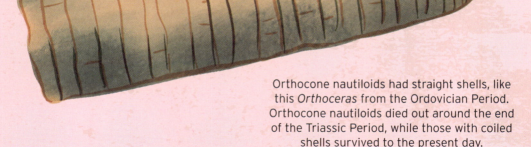

Orthocone nautiloids had straight shells, like this *Orthoceras* from the Ordovician Period. Orthocone nautiloids died out around the end of the Triassic Period, while those with coiled shells survived to the present day.

THE LIVING ORGANISM: *CAMEROCERAS*
Nautiloids were good swimmers that both scavenged and hunted for food. While most were just finger to arm length, the largest known nautiloid was *Cameroceras*, which had a shell that was 11 m (33 ft) long.

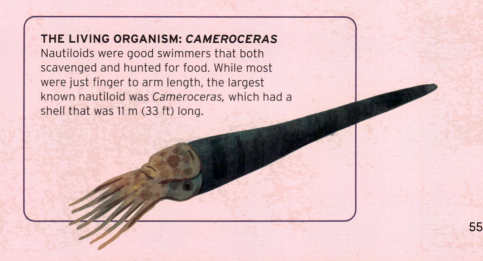

Ammonites

Ammonites were sea creatures that carried a shell. They were cephalopods, the same family as squid. Ammonites died out about 66 million years ago in the Cretaceous–Paleogene extinction event, at the same time as non-avian dinosaurs.

Pavlovia menneri

ORDER: Ammonitida
GROUP: Mollusk, Cephalopod
PERIOD: Early Jurassic–Early Paleogene, 200–66 million years ago
SIZE: 10 mm–3 m (0.4 in-10 ft) diameter
RARITY: Common

The shell was made of aragonite, the same mineral that pearls are made from.

The ammonite's flat spiral shell is divided into air chambers separated by walls called septa. These helped it stay buoyant underwater. New chambers would be added as the ammonite grew.

The animal lived in the last and largest chamber in the shell, the body chamber.

The thickness and structure of the ammonite's shell suggests it could survive water pressure at depths of up to 100 m (330 ft).

THE ANCIENT WORLD
Ammonites resemble today's nautiluses, and would probably have eaten plankton and crustaceans. They, in turn, became prey for ichthyosaurs (page 77) and mosasaurs.

GIANTS OF THE SEA
Ammonites range in size from species just 10 mm (0.4 in) across to giants as large as truck wheels. The largest specimen ever found was an incomplete example of *Parapuzosia seppenradensis*, with a diameter of 1.95 m (6.4 ft). Complete, it would have measured about 2.55 m (8.4 ft) across.

SNAKESTONES
Ammonites were first thought to be petrified coiled snakes. Collectors would sometimes carve a snake head at the end. The coat of arms for the UK coastal town of Whitby includes three snakestones.

Finding Ammonites

Ammonites may be found by splitting rocks. Look for pale gray limestone rocks along the hide-tide mark on the beach.

If you have permission to split an ammonite, wedge the rock between others to keep it in place. Place your chisel against the rock's thinner edge then give it a careful tap with your hammer to divide the ammonite into two halves.

Echinoids

Sea urchins and sand dollars belong in a group of echinoderms called echinoids that first appeared on Earth about 450 million years ago.

Temnocidaris intermedia

ORDER: Cidaroida
FAMILY: Cidaridae
PERIOD: Late Jurassic–Early Paleogene, 157–60 million years ago
SIZE: Up to 4.5 cm (1.8 in) diameter
RARITY: Common

Sea urchins preserve well as fossils, though the spines break away from their connecting tubercles after death, as seen on this *Temnocidaris* fossil from the Late Cretaceous Period. Complete specimens are very rare.

The shell of a sea urchin, called the test, is made of connecting plates made from the mineral calcite. Tests may be round, flat, or heart-shaped.

As well as working as a defense against predators, the spines had muscles attached so the urchin could move them like stilts to cross the sea bed.

THE LIVING ORGANISM: ECHINOIDS

Echinoids have rounded skeletons made of calcite plates, with alternating rows of defensive spines with perforated strips where tiny tube feet emerge. The spines sometimes contain a toxin. Sea urchins gnaw on algae through a mouth on their underside.

Irregular echinoids

Echinoids evolved during the Jurassic Period into flatter, burrowing animals called sand dollars and sea biscuits. Their disk-shaped skeletons are common finds on beaches.

Sea stars

Sea stars and brittle stars are fragile echinoderms that patrol the sea bed. Their five arms are used for gripping and feeling for food.

> **Pentasteria longispina**
>
> **ORDER:** Paxillosida
> **FAMILY:** Astropectinidae
> **PERIOD:** Early Jurassic–Early Cretaceous, 176–136 million years ago
> **SIZE:** 10 cm (4 in) diameter
> **RARITY:** Very rare

Sea stars do not last long after death so their fossils are very rare.

This fossil is of *Pentasteria*, a sea star from the Jurassic Period. Unlike modern-day sea stars, it did not have suckers on its arms that could break open the shells of its prey.

The skeleton is made up of small plates called ossicles that are the most usual parts of the sea star to be preserved.

BRITTLE STARS
Like sea stars, brittle stars have five arms but they are thin and delicate, surrounding a circular body. Brittle stars raise these arms to filter food from the sea. These fragile creatures rarely show up as fossils.

THE LIVING ORGANISM: SEA STARS
Sea stars, commonly known as starfish, usually have five arms featuring thousands of tiny tube feet around a mouth on their underside. The arms can easily be torn away and regrown. Sea stars are predators that feed mostly on bivalves (page 50) by pushing their stomachs into their prey's shell to consume them.

Chelicerates

Chelicerates are a group of arthropods without antennae. The group includes spiders, horseshoe crabs, and extinct species such as eurypterids, the so-called sea scorpions. Early chelicerates were marine creatures.

Eusarcana scorpionis

ORDER: Eurypterida
FAMILY: Eurypteridae
PERIOD: Silurian–Early Devonian, 433–412 million years ago
SIZE: 12 cm (4.8 in) in length
RARITY: Very rare

Most eurypterid fossils are actually the remains of exoskeletons that they shed when growing.

Paracarcinosoma was a eurypterid from the Silurian Period. The front limbs were pincers with sharp points on the inner edge.

Paracarcinosoma had claws, plus four pairs of legs for walking over the sea bed, and a sixth rear pair used for paddling.

PREHISTORIC RELIC
The modern-day living horseshoe crab is a relative of *Mesolimulus*, a chelicerate that lived from the Jurassic to the Cretaceous Period. The horseshoe crab has barely changed in 170 million years.

THE LIVING ORGANISM: EURYPTERIDS
These scorpion-like creatures lived mostly in fresh or slightly salty water. They ranged greatly in size. One of the largest, *Pterygotus*, may have reached 2.1 m (7 ft) in length. Eurypterids may have preyed on trilobites (page 44).

Weygoldtina was a tailless whip scorpion and relative of today's spiders. It lived in the shallow water of swamps during the Carboniferous Period.

Weygoldtina anglica

ORDER: Amblypygi
FAMILY: Weygoldtinidae
PERIOD: Carboniferous, 315–307 million years ago
SIZE: Up to 1.8 cm (0.5 in) in length
RARITY: Rare

Though it resembles a spider, *Weygoldtina* did not create silk or have venomous fangs.

The name Chelicerates means "claw-bearers" in reference to the small, grasping mouthparts, or chelicerae, these animals possess.

EIGHT LEGS AND MORE

A fossil of the arachnid *Chimerarachne yingi* was discovered in amber from Myanmar in 2018. Predating true spiders, this web-producing 100-million-year-old creature had eight legs, fangs, and feelers plus something extra—a tail. The tail is longer than its tiny, 2.5 mm (0.1 in) body and was possibly used to detect predators.

CAUGHT IN THE WEB

It is thought that early spiders began producing silk 400 million years ago. They used it to wrap and protect their eggs. Only later, when flying insects became more abundant during the Cretaceous Period, did spiders began to use silk to build webs and capture prey. Rare fossils of flies, beetles, and mites caught in spider silk have been preserved in amber.

Insects

Insects first appeared during the Ordovician Period on land and in fresh water. The first flying creatures on Earth were insects that evolved during the Devonian Period.

Meganeura monyi

ORDER: Meganisoptera
FAMILY: Meganeuridae
PERIOD: Late Carboniferous, 305–299 million years ago
SIZE: Up to 70 cm (27 in) wingspan
RARITY: Very rare

Despite their abundance, the fragility of insects means they are rarely fossilized in stone. Separated wings are most common, as they are often left uneaten by predators. Well-preserved examples of complete insects have been captured in amber, however.

Insects have an exoskeleton made of an amino sugar called chitin, which helps them avoid drying out.

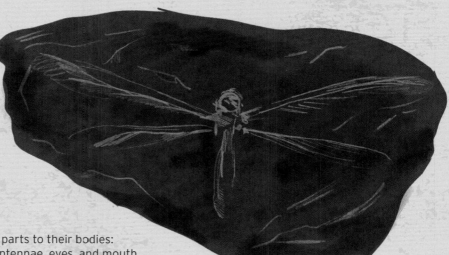

This large dragonfly-like *Meganaura* fossil was found in layers of coal from the Carboniferous Period.

Insects have three parts to their bodies:
- The **head**, with antennae, eyes, and mouth
- The **thorax**, which includes the legs and wings
- The **abdomen**, which contains the digestive and reproductive organs

THE ANCIENT WORLD
Unlike other arthropods, insects have three pairs of limbs. During the Carboniferous Period, when the atmosphere was rich in oxygen, some insects reached a great size, with the early dragonfly, *Meganaura*, having an impressive wingspan of 70 cm (27 in), almost five times that of the largest modern-day dragonfly. *Meganaura* would have preyed on other insects.

Archimylacris acadica

ORDER: Blattoptera
FAMILY: Archimylacridae
PERIOD: Late Carboniferous, 315–311 million years ago
SIZE: 3 cm (1.2 in) in length
RARITY: Very rare

Archimylacris was a Carboniferous ancestor of cockroaches, termites, and mantids. Like modern-day cockroaches it had a flattened body, head shield with long antennae, and folded wings.

Some prehistoric cockroaches grew to almost 30 cm (1 ft) in length.

The remains of cockroaches have been found as fossils from the prehistoric swamps where they lived on insects and rotting plants.

COLOSSAL CRAWLER
Millipedes are diplopodans rather than insects. Evidence of millipedes has been found dating back to the Devonian Period. Prehistoric millipedes include the largest known invertebrate, *Arthropleura armata*, a Late Carboniferous beast that could have measured 2.5 m (8 ft 2 in) in length. This crawled over Earth 100 million years before the dinosaurs.

63

CHAPTER 4: VERTEBRATES

The first vertebrates, or animals with backbones, were jawless fish that appeared in the Ordovician Period, about 480 million years ago. These were followed by amphibians that first stepped onto land in the Devonian. Reptiles of the Early Carboniferous evolved into both mammals and the dinosaurs that dominated the land for millions of years.

Jawless fish

The earliest fish had no jaws. They would have had to feed by sucking in small soft-bodied creatures and food debris.

Fossils of jawless fish are very rare, though incomplete examples have been found in some Devonian sites.

Pteraspis rostrata

ORDER: Pteraspidiformes
FAMILY: Pteraspididae
PERIOD: Devonian, 416–386 million years ago
SIZE: Up to 20 cm (8 in) in length
RARITY: Common

This partial fossil of *Pteraspis* preserves the bony plates protecting the front half of this flat-headed fish.

Pteraspis had a long, armored rostrum, or beak, in front of its tiny eyes.

THE LIVING ORGANISM: JAWLESS FISH
Jawless fish, sometimes called agnathans, began appearing in shallow waters during the Ordovician Period. They had bony armor and an internal flexible skeleton made of cartilage (the same material found in the human nose and ear). They did not have paired fins like modern fish.

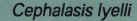
Cephalasis lyelli

ORDER: Osteostraci
FAMILY: Cephalaspidae
PERIOD: Early Devonian, 400 million years ago
SIZE: Up to 22 cm (8 in) in length
RARITY: Rare

This 400-million-year-old fossil shows the remains of an early fish called *Cephalasis lyelli*.

Cephalasis had a mouth on its underside. It browsed the sea bed without toothed jaws, feeding on soft-bodied creatures such as worms and shrimp.

The head is protected by bony armor. It is not known what may have preyed on jawless fish.

SURVIVING SUCKERS
Most jawless fish were wiped out during a major extinction event in the Late Devonian Period. There are a few modern-day survivors, however, in lampreys and hagfish. Lampreys feed by attaching themselves to the side of a dead fish like a parasite then rasping at its flesh with a circular mouth of tiny teeth. Eel-like hagfish feed on worms and the insides of rotting carcasses on the sea bed.

65

Jawed fish

The development of jaws allowed vertebrates to capture and bite into larger and tougher prey. It also provided the tools for grasping plants, digging, and making sounds.

Dunkleosteus terrelli

ORDER: Arthrodira
FAMILY: Dunkleosteidae
PERIOD: Late Devonian, 382–358 million years ago
SIZE: Up to 10 m (33 ft) in length
RARITY: Rare

Dunkleosteus was a huge fish with tough armor up to 5 cm (2 in) thick covering its head and jaws. It is this part that has survived in the fossil record.

Rather than separate teeth, *Dunkleosteus* had plates on its upper and lower jaw like blades. The top row wore down to form fangs.

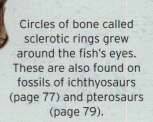

Circles of bone called sclerotic rings grew around the fish's eyes. These are also found on fossils of ichthyosaurs (page 77) and pterosaurs (page 79).

THE LIVING ORGANISM: *DUNKLEOSTEUS*
Arising in the Devonian Period, *Dunkleosteus* was the largest predator of its time. It was a placoderm, a primitive, armored, and jawed fish. Most placoderms were small bottom feeders. Instead of teeth they grew sharpened bony plates in their jaws that served the same function.

Fossilized shark teeth are by far the most common finds for collectors of early jawed vertebrates. Shark skeletons are made of cartilage, not bone, so they rarely fossilize. However, the teeth, along with spines in their fins, preserve well.

Otodus megaloden

ORDER: Lamniformes
FAMILY: Otodontidae
PERIOD: Neogene, 23–3.6 million years ago
SIZE: 18 m (59 ft) in length
RARITY: Common

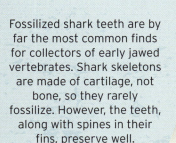

The discovery of megalodon bite marks in fossilized bones reveal that this predator was large enough to attack whales.

Sharks continually produce teeth to replace those that break or fall out, generating up to 40,000 in a lifetime.

The largest prehistoric shark teeth that can be found are those of *Otodus megalodon*. Megalodon means "big tooth." Its teeth measured up to 18 cm (7 in) long.

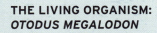

THE LIVING ORGANISM: *OTODUS MEGALODON*

Sharks first appeared in the Late Devonian Period and survived major extinction periods through to the present day. At 18 m (59 ft), *Otodus megalodon* was three times the length of the largest great white shark today. This giant of the seas became extinct about 3.6 million years ago, when the planet began to cool.

Bony fish

Unlike sharks and jawless fish, osteichthyes, or bony fish, have skeletons mostly made of bone. Today these make up the largest group of fish.

Knightia eoceaena

ORDER: Clupeiformes
FAMILY: Clupeidae
PERIOD: Paleogene, 50 million years ago
SIZE: Up to 25 cm (10 in) in length
RARITY: Common

Knightia eoceaena is commonly found in freshwater sediments in the Green River region in Wyoming, USA, and has become the state's official fossil.

Knightia was prey to many larger fish and has been found in the fossilized stomachs of several species.

With skeletons made of bone, more complete bodies of osteichthyes are preserved as fossils, compared to placoderms and sharks with skeletons made of cartilage (page 66).

This ray-finned fish has fins supported by parallel rows of bony spines. Ray-finned fish are the most diverse class of vertebrates alive today.

THE LIVING ORGANISM: KNIGHTIA
This herring-like freshwater bony fish evolved in the middle of the Paleogene Period, about 50 million years ago. *Knightia* lived in schools, as revealed by fossil layers that include thousands grouped together.

Xiphactinus audax

ORDER: Ichthyodectiformes
FAMILY: Ichthyodectidae
PERIOD: Late Cretaceous, 100–66 million years ago
SIZE: 6 m (20 ft) in length
RARITY: Common

Xiphactinus was a large predatory fish with a backbone made up of over 100 vertebrae.

Despite its size, *Xiphactinus* was the not the top marine predator of its time. It has been found in the preserved remains of the even larger Cretaceous Period shark *Cretoxyrhina*.

This fossil from the Sternberg Museum of Natural History in Kansas, USA, shows a 2 m (6.5 ft) fish called *Gillicus arcuatus* captured in the *Xiphactinus*'s belly.

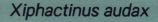

Lost and found

The coelacanth was a bony fish that fossils recorded as living 410 million years ago. It was thought to have died out in the Late Cretaceous Period, 66 million years ago. Then, in 1938, it was found alive in waters off the South African coast. More examples have since been found off the coasts of East Africa and Indonesia.

THE LIVING ORGANISM: *XIPHACTINUS*
In comparison with tiny *Knightia*, *Xiphactinus* was a monster, the largest known bony fish. Growing up to 6 m (20 ft) long, this fanged hunter lived through the second half of the Cretaceous Period from about 100 million years ago. A powerful swimmer, it could have chased prey rather than attempt ambushes.

Amphibians

Amphibians were the first vertebrates to adapt to life on land, over 400 million years ago. While they could explore and hunt on land, they laid and hatched their eggs in water.

Eryops megacephalus

ORDER: Temnospondyli
FAMILY: Eryopidae
PERIOD: Permian, 299–278 million years ago
SIZE: Up to 2 m (6 ft) in length
RARITY: Rare

Fossils of *Eryops* have been found in Texas, USA, in sediment from prehistoric swamps. Unlike most amphibians, *Eryops* had a complete skeleton of bone, which meant it preserved well.

At a maximum of 2 m (6 ft) *Eryops* was slightly longer than today's largest amphibian, the Chinese giant salamander.

As with most amphibians, *Eryops* had four toes on its front feet and five on its rear feet.

Eryops's ribs were straight and did not form a cage, as they do on reptiles and mammals.

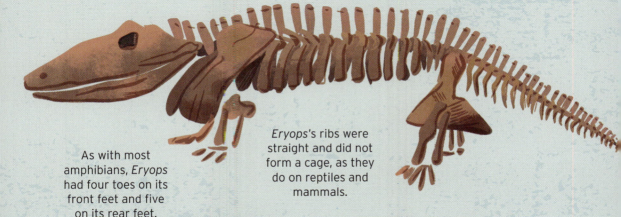

THE LIVING ORGANISM: *ERYOPS*
Amphibians evolved from extinct lobe-finned fish called rhipidistians. One of the largest land animals of its time, *Eryops* was a flat-headed amphibian that resembled a crocodile, with eyes and nostrils on the top of its head. It would have divided its time between land and water. Like many large prehistoric amphibians, *Eryops* became extinct by the end of the Triassic Period.

Diplocaulus had short legs similar to those of modern-day newts. It probably relied more on its whiplike tail to propel it through water.

Diplocaulus magnicornis

ORDER: Nectridea
FAMILY: Diplocaulidae
PERIOD: Late Carboniferous–Permian, 306–255 million years ago
SIZE: Up to 1 m (3.3 ft) in length
RARITY: Rare

FROM SEA TO LAND
Tiktaalik was a large bony fish from the Late Devonian Period with a flattened head and stiff fins that it could have used to pull itself onto land. It is one of the earliest examples of a fish developing into an amphibian. The first *Tiktaalik* fossils were found in Nunavut, Canada, in 2002.

The odd shape of *Diplocaulus*'s head may have helped it cut through water, like a plane's wings through air, or it may have worked as a defense, making the creature too wide for most predators to swallow.

THE LIVING ORGANISM: *DIPLOCAULUS*
Described as a giant Permian newt, *Diplocaulus* was one of the most unusual-looking early amphibians, with a wide, arrow-shaped head. Up to 1 m (3.3 ft) in length, *Diplocaulus* lived in rivers and lakes from the Late Carboniferous to the Late Permian Period.

Early reptiles

Reptiles were descendants of a branch of amphibians, adapted to life on land, with dry, scaly skin. From the group would come snakes, turtles, lizards, crocodilians, and the largest creatures to walk the Earth—the dinosaurs.

Hylonomus lyelli

ORDER: Captorhinidae
FAMILY: Protorothyrididae
PERIOD: Carboniferous, 315–311 million years ago
SIZE: Up to 20 cm (8 in) in length
RARITY: Very rare

Hylonomus lyelli remains have been found in cliffs in Nova Scotia, Canada, within the fossilized stumps of scale trees (page 30) where they may have sought out prey.

As shown in this fossil of a *Hylonomus* jaw, this reptile had rows of many sharp teeth. It is likely these were used to catch insects.

The ability of reptiles to lay eggs away from water freed them to explore inland and take over forests and higher ground. Their eggs are called amniote eggs, and had a shell that let air pass through but retained liquids and a yolk for the embryo to feed on. This allowed young reptiles to develop without a larval stage in water, and reduced the risk of young being eaten by predators.

THE LIVING ORGANISM: *HYLONOMUS LYELLI*

This small creature from the Late Carboniferous Period is the oldest confirmed reptile. *Hylonomus lyelli* grew to about 20 cm (8 in) long, including the tail. It resembled a lizard, though lizards would not appear on Earth for millions more years (page 75).

REMOTE COUSIN

The tuatara is a relic of the Triassic Period. This lizard-like animal is actually a primitive reptile called a rhynchocephalian, the only one to survive into the present day. It did so by being separated from competition with other animals when New Zealand split from Antarctica over 66 million years ago, in the Cretaceous Period. The tuatara is now a protected species and is hugely important to experts on evolution.

Turtles

Turtles began to evolve from the Permian Period with wide ribs and a backbone that would eventually fuse to become a shell. By the Late Triassic, recognizable turtles roamed the Earth, with complete shells that the turtles could withdraw inside.

Stylemys nebrascensis

ORDER: Testudines
FAMILY: Testudinidae
PERIOD: Paleogene, 40–13 million years ago
SIZE: Up to 1 m (3.3 ft) in length
RARITY: Rare

The heavy bones and shells of turtles preserve well as fossils, though most shells are found as fragments. The shell grew with the tortoise.

Turtle skulls include large eye sockets. Turtles do not have teeth but beak-like jaws for tearing plants.

This fossil shows the rounded back shell, or carapace, above the flatter belly shell, or plastron, of a common tortoise called *Stylemys nebrascensis*.

THE LIVING ORGANISM: *STYLEMYS*
This tortoise lived in the Mid Paleogene Period. Tortoises live on land rather than both land and water, as turtles do. *Stylemys* was likely a plant-eater, using its beak-like jaws to tear and chew leaves. The shell was covered with an outer layer of scales called scutes, that were made of keratin, the same material in our fingernails.

The largest-ever freshwater turtle was the species *Stupendemys geographica*. A spectacular fossilized shell of this reptile from the Neogene Period measures 2.9 m (9.4 ft) long.

Crocodilians

Crocodilians evolved during the Late Triassic, about 225 million years ago. Small, long-legged reptiles grew into shorter-limbed, long-snouted predators with bony armor and powerful bites. Some were giants that could take on dinosaurs.

Deinosuchus riograndenis

ORDER: Crocodilia
FAMILY: Alligatoroidea
PERIOD: Late Cretaceous, 82–73 million years ago
SIZE: 10.6 m (35 ft) in length
RARITY: Rare

Deinosuchus means "terror crocodile." Despite its name, *Deinosuchus riograndenis* was from the alligator family, one of the largest ever, weighing up to 9 tonnes (10 tons).

Crocodilians have nostrils on the top and end of their snout so they can breathe air while remaining mostly hidden just below the water's surface.

THE LIVING ORGANISM: CROCODILIANS

Prehistoric crocodilians lived on coasts and in the oceans. Land crocodilians probably hunted in a similar way to present-day survivors, attacking prey from shallow water then drowning it. *Deinosuchus riograndenis* may have been the largest ancient crocodile, twice the size of the modern-day saltwater crocodile. While surviving crocodiles rarely venture into open ocean, marine crocodiles were common in the Jurassic and Cretaceous Period, with *Steneosaurus* a known open-water fish hunter.

ARMOR PLATING

Crocodilians' tough skin features rows of armor-like bones along the back and tail. These are called osteoderms. Examples of this underskin plating are commonly discovered as fossils. Osteoderms are also found in some species of lizard, frog, and dinosaur.

Lizards

Lizards date back to the Late Triassic Period. They are common, mostly carnivorous reptiles with scaly skin and forked tongues that they use to detect scents in the air.

Megalania prisca

ORDER: Squamata
FAMILY: Varanidae
PERIOD: Neogene, 1.5 million–40,000 years ago
SIZE: Up to 7 m (23 ft) in length
RARITY: Very rare

Megalania prisca was a lizard whose fossil was found in Australia. It was named in 1859 when three large fossilized vertebrae were received by the famous English paleontologist Sir Richard Owen at the British Museum.

This fossil of a *Megalania prisca* upper jawbone measures 22 cm (9 in) in length.

Who me?

Ancient encounters between Aboriginal Australians and *Megalania prisca* may have inspired legends of encounters with giant lizards, including the Whowie, a huge cave-dwelling goanna with six frog-shaped legs.

THE LIVING ORGANISM: *MEGALANIA PRISCA*

The oldest true lizard fossils date from the Late Jurassic Period. Complete lizard fossils are rare, but bones can be found. The giant monitor *Megalania prisca* was the largest known land lizard, twice the size of today's Komodo dragon. It was a powerful predator capable of attacking huge marsupials. It became extinct at the time humans arrived on Australia, about 40,000 years ago.

Snakes

During the Cretaceous Period some burrowing and marine lizards began to lose their limbs and evolved into snakes, including one species that grew longer than a modern-day school bus.

Titanoboa cerrejonensis

ORDER: Squamata
FAMILY: Boidae
PERIOD: Paleogene, 60–58 million years ago
SIZE: 13 m (42 ft) in length
RARITY: Very rare

Fossil traces of land snakes are very rare. This vertebra was found in a coal mine in Colombia.

Experts estimate that this bone belonged to an ancient anaconda that grew up to 13 m (42 ft) long, the largest snake ever, with a suitable name, *Titanoboa cerrejonensis*.

Study of the giant snake's skull bones shows gaps between closely packed teeth, which suggest it preyed on fish as well as the turtles and crocodilians found among its fossil remains.

THE LIVING ORGANISM: *TITANOBOA CERREJONENSIS*

Snakes appeared at the end of the Cretaceous Period and may have evolved from burrowing lizards or sea snakes. About 58 million years ago, the enormous *Titanoboa cerrejonensis* evolved, the largest snake to have ever lived. It grew to 13 m (42 ft) long and lived in rain forests.

Ichthyosaurs

Ichthyosaurs were air-breathing marine reptiles that resembled dolphins. Originating in the Triassic Period, they are among some of the most famous fossil finds in history.

Stenopterygius quadriscissus

ORDER: Ichthyosauria
FAMILY: Stenopterygiidae
PERIOD: Late Triassic–Early Cretaceous, 216–122 million years ago
SIZE: Up to 3.3 m (10.8 ft) in length
RARITY: Rare

The first complete fossilized skeletons of ichthyosaurs were discovered in England in the early nineteenth century.

Some ichthyosaur fossils found in Germany include the outline of flesh around the bones, along with skin that shows that ichthyosaurs were smooth rather than scaly.

The bones in the ichthyosaur's paddles clearly show what would once have been individual digits.

The discovery of ichthyosaur fossils carrying embryos revealed that these marine reptiles gave birth to live young.

In search of treasure

One of the most famous fossil hunters was Mary Anning, who explored the coastline of southwest England for fossils in the early nineteenth century. At the age of 12, along with her brother, Joseph, she discovered a 5 m (16.5 ft)-long skeleton in the cliffs, the first evidence of an ichthyosaur. She later found the first fossil of a plesiosaur (page 78). The area in Dorset, England, where she found her treasures is now referred to as the Jurassic Coast and is a popular spot for amateur fossil hunters.

THE LIVING ORGANISM: *ICTHYOSAURUS*

This fast-swimming predator had a long jaw full of fine, sharp teeth, ideal for grabbing fish and squid. *Ichthyosaurus*'s tai fins were vertical like a fish, rather than horizontal like modern-day dolphins and whales. *Ichthyosaurus* had large eyes, which suggests they often hunted in deep and murky water.

Plesiosaurs

The largest marine reptiles in history were the plesiosaurs. Plesiosaurs had small heads and extraordinarily long necks to help them reach food, while the related pliosaurs had large heads and jaws and caught much larger prey.

> **Thalassiodracon hawkinsi**
>
> ORDER: Plesiosauria
> FAMILY: Plesiosauridae
> PERIOD: Late Triassic–Early Jurassic, 200–199 million years ago
> SIZE: Up to 2 m (6.6 ft) in length
> RARITY: Rare

Plesiosaur remains are among the earliest recognized reptile fossils. Their fossil vertebrae are recorded from 1605, though they were then thought be parts of ancient fish.

The remains of plesiosaurs, like this small *Thalassiodracon hawkinsi*, are found in rocks from the Jurassic Period in Europe and Cretaceous Period rocks in the North American Great Plains.

The plesiosaur *Albertonectes vanderveldei* had a neck with 76 vertebrae, more than any other known vertebrate ever.

THE LIVING ORGANISM: PLESIOSAURS

While dinosaurs roamed the land, plesiosaurs shared the oceans with fellow air-breathers, the ichthyosaurs (page 77). Plesiosaurs used their four paddle-like limbs to swim slowly, then reached for food using their necks which were sometimes longer than their body. They fed on fish and mollusks. Plesiosaurs died out during the huge extinction event at the end of the Cretaceous Period.

Pliosaurs did not have the plesiosaurs' long neck but they made up for it with large jaws and bulk. The largest, *Kronosaurus*, reached 11 m (36 ft) in length. It is found n Australian rocks from the Cretaceous Period.

Pterosaurs

Pterosaurs were the first flying vertebrates, long before birds and bats took to the air. The front limbs of these reptiles evolved into wings with a membrane stretched wide between their extended fourth fingers and ankles. Some grew impressive head crests.

Pterodactylus antiquus

ORDER: Pterosauria
FAMILY: Pterodactylidae
PERIOD: Late Jurassic, 150–148 million years ago
SIZE: Up to 1 m (3.5 ft) wingspan
RARITY: Very rare

Pterosaurs had hollow bones like modern-day birds, which are fragile and rarely preserved. *Pterodactylus antiquus* had a crest made of soft tissue. This rarely survives fossilization.

The fossil is of *Pterodactylus antiquus*, a small pterosaur from the Late Jurassic Period with a wingspan of about 1 m (3.5 ft). It had about 90 needle-like teeth in its long jaws.

Detailed fossils from Solnhofen in Germany, Kazakhstan, and China have revealed that pterosaurs were covered with fine hair, called pycnofibers, which suggested they were warm-blooded.

THE LIVING ORGANISM: PTEROSAURS

The fossilized remains of pterosaurs, like *Pterodactylus antiquus*, are found in lake or seabed sediments, which suggests they preyed on fish, scooping them up while flying just above the water's surface or diving in like pelicans. Inland, forest-dwelling pterosaurs are likely to have caught insects. These were small, the size of pigeons. The largest of all the pterosaurs was *Quetzalcoatlus northropi*. At 11 m (36 ft) it had a wingspan similar to that of a small plane.

Bird-hipped dinosaurs

Dinosaurs are split into two groups: saurischia, reptile-hipped dinosaurs; and ornithischia, bird-hipped dinosaurs. The bird-hipped dinosaurs were mostly plant-eaters and include dinosaurs with armor, frills, and horns.

Euoplocephalus tutus

ORDER: Ornithischia
FAMILY: Ankylosauridae
PERIOD: Late Cretaceous, 76–70 million years ago
SIZE: 6 m (20 ft) in length
RARITY: Very rare

Euoplocephalus tutus lived in the Late Cretaceous Period in what is now Canada. It measured an average 6 m (20 ft) in length and weighed 2 tonnes (2.2 tons).

This fossil of a *Euoplocephalus tutus* club includes a sample of the dinosaur's skin, preserved on its tail.

More than 40 almost-complete fossilized skeletons of *Euoplocephalus tutus* exist, complete with the bony spikes called scutes that covered its back, and the heavy club on the end of its tail. This club would have been swung toward attackers.

THE LIVING ORGANISM: ORNITHISCHIANS
Early ornithischians were small, long-tailed dinosaurs that could run fast on two legs. Some developed into bulky four-legged reptiles, such as the armored ankylosaurs, like *Euoplocephalus tutus*, and the plated stegosaurs, both of which wielded tails with a hammer or spikes for defense.

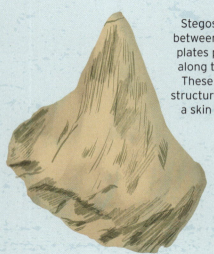

Stegosaurs had between 17 and 22 plates positioned along their back. These are bony structures that had a skin covering.

Stegosaurus ungulatus

ORDER: Ornithischia
FAMILY: Stegosauridae
PERIOD: Late Jurassic, 159–144 million years ago
SIZE: Up to 7.5 m (23 ft) in length
RARITY: Very rare

When first unearthed, the plates from a *Stegosaurus* were thought to lie flat and overlap on the animal's back. Following the discovery of near-complete skeletons, the plates are now known to be positioned upright from the neck to the tail.

The plates, up to 60 cm (23.5 in) tall, are understood to have been covered in horn or skin, and used either for defense or to communicate with other stegosaurs, or possibly to help regulate body temperature.

IT'S IN THE HIP
The key difference between saurischia and ornithischia is the positioning of their pelvic bones. Saurischia (above) had a pubis pointing forward while ornithischia (below) had a pubis directed toward the tail. Despite ornithischia being described as bird-hipped dinosaurs, they are not related to birds. Birds evolved from a branch of the reptile-hipped dinosaurs, saurischia.

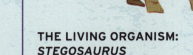

THE LIVING ORGANISM: *STEGOSAURUS*
Stegosaurus lived around 150 million years ago in North America and Europe. This bulky herbivore had a relatively small head and brain. It would have browsed on low vegetation, grinding plants between its back teeth. Long spikes on its tail were a useful defense against predators such as *Allosaurus*.

Reptile-hipped dinosaurs

Saurischia, the reptile-hipped dinosaurs, are made up of two main types: theropods, which include predators such as *T. rex;* and sauropods, giant long-necked dinosaurs, the largest creatures to ever walk the Earth.

> ### *Argentinosaurus huinculensis*
> **CLADE:** Saurischia
> **CLADE:** Titanosauridae
> **PERIOD:** Late Cretaceous, 96–92 million years ago
> **SIZE:** Up to 34 m (112 ft) in length
> **RARITY:** Very rare

The fossilized thigh bone, or femur, for *Argentinosaurus huinculensis* measures 2.5 m (8.2 ft) high, much taller than an adult human.

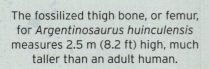

The size of the sauropod *Argentinosaurus huinculensis* has been calculated based on a limited number of fossil remains, including nine vertebrae, partial leg bones, and ribs.

THE LIVING ORGANISM: SAUROPODS
Sauropods were large plant-eaters, including possibly the largest animal ever to walk on land, *Argentinosaurus huinculensis*, a Late Cretaceous titanosaur that grew up to 34 m (112 ft) in length from head to tip of tail. The sauropods were able to use their long neck to reach high tree foliage. Like modern-day cattle, the sauropods needed large guts to digest plant matter. They swallowed stones, called gastroliths, to grind the food in their stomachs. These smoothed stones sometimes turn up among fossils.

This fossilized tooth found in Canada belonged to a tyrannosaur that lived in the Late Cretaceous Period.

Tyrannosaurus rex

CLADE: Saurischia
FAMILY: Tyrannosauridae
PERIOD: Late Cretaceous, 68–66 million years ago
SIZE: Up to 12.4 m (40.7 ft) in length
RARITY: Very rare

Tyrannosaurus rex had between 50 and 60 such teeth, up to 30 cm (12 in) long, as large as bananas. As its teeth wore down or broke they were replaced by new ones.

On the inside of the tooth are fine serrations that helped the predator cut through flesh like a steak knife.

T. rex bite marks have been found on the fossilized remains of the plant-eater *Triceratops*.

THE LIVING ORGANISM: THEROPODS
Theropods were carnivores that walked on two legs. These range from the pigeon-sized *Microraptor zhaoianus* to the fearsome 12.4 m (40.7 ft)-long *Tyrannosaurus rex*. *T. rex* was a fast predator and scavenger with short forearms but a large head with jaws that could produce a bite force of 6 tonnes (6.5 tons) and crush bone. The tyrannosaurs and sauropods all died out about 66 million years ago following what is understood to be the impact of a huge asteroid in the Yucatan Peninsula of Mexico.

Birds

The only dinosaurs to have survived the extinction event at the end of the Cretaceous Period are birds. These warm-blooded vertebrates with feathered wings first appeared about 70 million years ago, with one bird-like dinosaur appearing 80 million years earlier.

Archaeopteryx siemensii

CLADE: Saurischia
FAMILY: Archaeopterygidae
PERIOD: Late Jurassic, 150–148 million years ago
SIZE: Up to 50 cm (20 in) in length
RARITY: Very rare

The fragile nature of birds' hollow bones and the softness of feathers means that bird fossils are extremely rare.

Fossilized *Archaeopteryx* remains have only been found in the limestone of Germany's Solnhofen region. These include the imprints of feathers.

While not a direct ancestor of modern-day birds, the 147-million-year-old *Archaeopteryx* is proof of the link between dinosaurs and birds.

This early bird probably used its claws to climb trees then glided between treetops.

FEATHERED FOSSILS
Highly detailed Early Cretaceous fossils from Liaoning, China, unearthed from 1996, revealed that many dinosaurs, such as this *Sinosauropteryx*, had a coat of downy feathers like modern-day chicks. These would have kept them warm. The feathers may have been brightly colored, though color does not easily survive the fossilization process. Further discoveries suggest some tyrannosaurs may have sported simple feathers.

THE LIVING ORGANISM: *ARCHAEOPTERYX*
A predecessor of modern birds, *Archaeopteryx* was a raven-sized dinosaur from the Late Jurassic Period. While it had feathered wings, it also had claws on its winged limbs, a bony tail, and teeth in its beak. It died out about 150 million years ago. Modern-day birds evolved from theropod dinosaurs about 80 million years later.

Proto-mammals

The synapsids proceeded mammals in Earth's history. They were once called mammal-like reptiles, though they were not related to reptiles.

Cynognathus crateronotus

CLADE: Synapsida
FAMILY: Cynognathidae
PERIOD: Mid Triassic, 247–237 million years ago
SIZE: Up to 1.2 m (4 ft) in length
RARITY: Very rare

Synapsids are named for holes in their skulls behind their eye sockets.

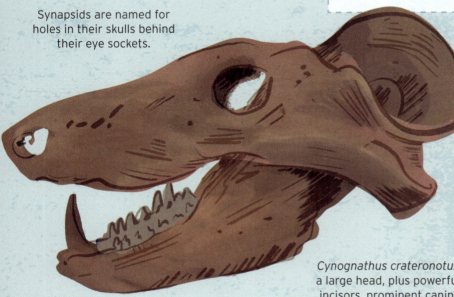

Strong jaw muscles would have been attached to the skull just behind the eye sockets.

Cynognathus crateronotus was a synapsid with a large head, plus powerful jaws featuring front incisors, prominent canine teeth, and serrated teeth in the cheeks. This means it could break up and chew food before swallowing.

THE LIVING ORGANISM: *CYNOGNATHUS*

Synapsids were meat- and plant-eaters that first appeared about 300 million years ago. They were the most common large land animals before dinosaurs took over. Some synapsids survived to become the ancestors of mammals. *Cynognathus* was a wolf-sized carnivore that lived on semi-arid land from the Early Triassic. It may have sported a coat of fur. The name *Cynognathus* is based on the Greek for "dog jaw."

Early mammals

Mammals, including humans, evolved from creatures that first appeared in the Late Triassic Period, when they were mostly small creatures that lived in the shadow of dinosaurs. Unlike reptiles, mammals produce milk for their young and have fur or hair.

Megazostrodon rudnerae

ORDER: Morganucodonta
FAMILY: Megazostrodontidae
PERIOD: Late Triassic, 200 million years ago
SIZE: Up to 12 cm (4.7 in) in length
RARITY: Very rare

Megazostrodon rudnerae is an early mammal known from fossils unearthed in Southern Africa.

Its skull had a relatively large brain case. *Megazostrodon* is thought to have had a good sense of hearing and smell.

This tiny animal had a rat-like tail and feet with five toes.

EARLY MAMMALS

The first true mammals were shrew-sized creatures, such as *Megazostrodon* from the Late Triassic Period. *Megazostrodon* grew up to about 12 cm (4.7 in) long. Its large eyes suggest it was nocturnal, hunting insects at night when it could avoid dinosaur predators. As a warm-blooded mammal, *Megazostrodon* could generate its own heat from the food it ate and be active during the coldest hours. It is thought that *Megazostrodon* laid eggs rather than giving birth to live young.

The unusual shape at the front of the *Diprotodon* skull is where it grew large nostrils or supported a short trunk, like that of a modern-day tapir.

Diprotodon optatum

ORDER: Diprotodontia
FAMILY: Diprotodontidae
PERIOD: Quaternary, 1.8 million–40,000 years ago
SIZE: Up to 4 m (13 ft) in length
RARITY: Rare

One preserved *Diprotodon* skeleton bears the mark of a spear, suggesting these huge plant-eaters were hunted by humans.

Diprotodon's name means "two forward teeth." There was a long gap between the *Diprotodon*'s forward-pointing incisors and its rear chewing teeth.

Grouped fossils suggest *Diprotodon* formed family groups. Many fossilized remains have been found around Lake Callabonna in South Australia, where the creatures were caught in mud as the lake dried out.

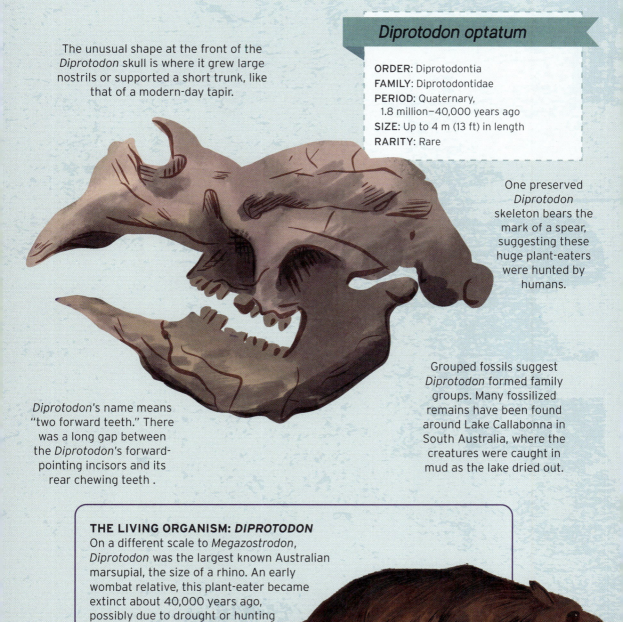

THE LIVING ORGANISM: *DIPROTODON*
On a different scale to *Megazostrodon*, *Diprotodon* was the largest known Australian marsupial, the size of a rhino. An early wombat relative, this plant-eater became extinct about 40,000 years ago, possibly due to drought or hunting by humans. As a marsupial, female *Diprotodon* gave birth to immature young that developed in a pouch, where they were fed on their mother's milk.

Creodonts

During the Paleogene, following the extinction of non-avian dinosaurs, new meat-eating mammals took their place as the chief land predators.

Hyaenodon horridus

ORDER: Hyaenodonta
FAMILY: Hyaenodontidae
PERIOD: Paleogene-Neocene, 42–16.9 million years ago
SIZE: 2 m (6.5 ft) in length
RARITY: Very rare

Hyaenodon ("hyena tooth") had a large skull but a small brain. *Hyaenodon* species ranged in size from that of a modern-day stoat to tiger-sized predators.

Their tooth marks have been found in early horses, camels, and even other predators.

Despite the name, *Hyaenodon* is not an ancestor of the modern-day hyena, which is more closely related to cats.

THE LIVING ORGANISM: CREODONTS

Creodonts, such as *Hyaenodon*, resembled hyenas, wolves, and wolverines. The largest was the bear-like *Megistotherium*, which grew to 3.5 m (11.5 ft) in length. Creodonts declined in numbers at the same time the order Carnivora became dominant. They may have competed for the same food and territory. The last creodont, *Dissopsalis*, from north Asia, died out about 9 million years ago.

Carnivorous mammals

The order Carnivora includes flesh-eating mammals such as weasels, foxes, wolves, cats, and bears. These became the dominant land predators from the Early Paleogene Period.

> **Smilodon fatalis**
>
> ORDER: Carnivora
> FAMILY: Felidae
> PERIOD: Quaternary, 2.5 million–10,000 years ago
> SIZE: Up to 1.7 m (5.5 ft) in length
> RARITY: Uncommon

The remains of hundreds of *Smilodon fatalis*, the saber-toothed cat, have been found preserved in the La Brea Tar Pits in Los Angeles, USA.

The saber teeth of the *Smilodon* were serated along the rear edge to help them slice through flesh.

Many of the bones found in La Brea show signs of repaired fractures or arthritis. The survival of these animals suggests that these cats lived in groups that supported wounded individuals.

THE LIVING ORGANISM: *SMILODON*
The first Carnivora were small ferret-sized creatures. Over several million years Carnivora grew into large and diverse predators. The saber-toothed cat, *Smilodon*, was almost the size of a modern-day lion, with a short tail and distinct canine teeth, which measured up to 28 cm (11 in) in length. Its jaws could open wide to about 120 degrees, allowing the cat to use its long teeth to stab prey. *Smilodon* hunted large plant-eaters such as camels and bison in the Americas. It is not known if *Smilodon* had a patterned coat or not. This muscular predator became extinct about 10,000 years ago, possibly due to climate change and a reduction in available prey.

Horses

From the Paleogene Period, horses developed from dog-sized herbivores into the fleet-footed, hoofed, and domesticated animals of the present day.

Mesohippus barbouri

ORDER: Perissodactyla
FAMILY: Equidae
PERIOD: Paleogene, 37–32 million years ago
SIZE: 60 cm (24 in) height
RARITY: Rare

Horses evolved from many-toed mammals into animals with one hoofed toe on each foot about 50 million years ago.

Mesohippus was an early hoof-less horse, the height of a large dog. It fed on twigs and fruit.

It had three toes on the foot of each long leg, with the middle toe considerably larger than the other two. This bore most of the animal's weight. This development was part way to the eventual single toe and hoof of modern-day horses.

Horses developed high-crowned teeth to cope with grinding leaves and grass. These teeth are the most commonly found fossil remains of early equids in North American Ice Age layers.

THE LIVING ORGANISM: HORSES
The first horses, like *Mesohippus*, were small, about the size of a dog. Horses are grazers, alert and quick to race away from danger. Ancient horses are also recorded in early Stone Age cave paintings.

Large herbivores

The Ice Age that lasted from about 2.5 million to 11,700 years ago saw the rise of giant herbivores. The mammoths were the largest of them all and became prey for early human hunters.

Mammuthus primigenius

ORDER: Proboscidea
FAMILY: Elephantidae
PERIOD: Neogene–Quaternary, 5 million–4,500 years ago
SIZE: 4 m (13 ft) height
RARITY: Rare

This fossil find is a 30 cm (1 ft)-long mammoth molar, a tooth from the animal's cheek used for grinding plant matter. A typical mammoth would go through six sets of teeth through its life.

The tooth is made up of plates made from a material called dentine, which is covered with enamel.

The evolution of mammoth species can be traced through the development of their teeth and the increasing number of enamel ridges on their molars.

THE LIVING ORGANISM: MAMMOTHS

About 10 different species of mammoths roamed the Earth during the Neogene Period. The 3.5 m (11.5 ft)-high, small-eared woolly mammoth populated the northern continents, with a shaggy coat to protect it from the cold. Its curled tusks were longer than those of modern-day elephants and may have proved useful in clearing snow to find plants. These giants of the Ice Age were hunted by early humans, who used their tusks as frames for buildings, tools, and ornaments. The last surviving mammoth was a dwarf species that died on Wrangel Island, Russia, approximately 4,500 years ago.

Frozen finds

As changing climate melts the permafrost in Siberia, many mummified mammoth remains have come to light, including whole specimens with skin and fur. Scientists have recovered DNA from these mammoth remains and confirmed their relationship to modern-day elephants.

Marine mammals

Life made its way onto land over 420 million years ago. Then, about 170 million years later, some reptiles moved back to the water, evolving into ichthyosaurs and plesiosaurs (pages 77–78). Some mammals followed about 53 million years ago, resulting in cetaceans and the largest animal to ever exist on Earth, the blue whale.

Basilosaurus cetoides

ORDER: Artiodactyla
FAMILY: Basilosauridae
PERIOD: Paleogene, 41–34 million years ago
SIZE: Up to 20 m (66 ft) in length
RARITY: Rare

This fossilized *Basilosaurus* skeleton reveals four limbs with knees. While retaining bone joints and digits, both pairs of limbs had evolved into swimming paddles.

Compared with modern-day whales, *Basilosaurus* had a small head for its body size.

Basilosaurus teeth are varied and reptile-like. This primitive whale could crunch on bone and chew its food, unlike modern cetaceans, which swallow their food whole.

THE LIVING ORGANISM: CETACEANS

The earliest known ancestor of cetaceans (whales and dolphins) was a tiny deer-like mammal called *Indohyus* that moved into the water about 50 million years ago. Over millions of years, these marine mammals developed paddles and a wide tail for swimming efficiently. *Basilosaurus* ("king lizard") was an early whale-type mammal found in the ancient oceans from about 41 million years ago. At up to 20 m (66 ft) in length, it preyed on large fish, including sharks.

Primates

Apes, monkeys, and humans are descended from primates that evolved on Earth following the extinction of most dinosaurs.

Darwinius masillae

ORDER: Primates
FAMILY: Adapidae
PERIOD: Mid Paleogene, 47 million years ago
SIZE: Up to 58 cm (23 in) in length
RARITY: Very rare

This early primate fossil, about 95 percent complete, shows a female *Darwinius masillae*, named after the naturalist Charles Darwin.

The fossil, nicknamed Ida, was discovered in a disused quarry near Frankfurt, Germany, in 1983 and is the best-preserved early primate fossil found to date.

The large eye sockets in the skull suggest *Darwinius* was a nocturnal creature.

The remains of a fruit and leaf diet were found in her stomach.

THE LIVING ORGANISM: PRIMATES

Primates began as small mammals that were adapted to life in trees in tropical forests, with hands and feet designed for gripping. Some developed opposable thumbs. Instead of claws, they grew nails and their eyes were forward-facing. Primate brains were generally larger than those in mammals of a similar size. *Darwinius* was an early primate from about 47 million years ago. This lemur-like creature is thought to be an ancestor of both lemurs and lorises.

Hominins

Modern-day humans, *Homo sapiens*, are the last in a series of hominins that arose some 7 million years ago. Some hominin species are our direct ancestors, but many branched off and became extinct.

Trace fossils of hominin footprints were found in rock in Laotoli, Tanzania, in 1976. The prints, preserved by a layer of volcanic ash, have been dated to 3.7 million years ago. The species that left these prints is thought to be *Australopithecus aferensis*.

There are several footprints trails in the rock, two walking in a line next to smaller prints to the right. It has been suggested that these were left by a family group.

Australopithecus aferensis

ORDER: Primates
FAMILY: Hominidae
PERIOD: Neogene,
 3.9–2.9 million years ago
SIZE: Average 1.5 m (5 ft) height
RARITY: Very rare

The trace fossils can tell us a lot about the people that passed this way. The prints are clearly made by early humans, as the big toes are in line with the rest of the toes, unlike those of apes.

The impression of the heel in the rock is deeper than the toes, which shows these hominins walked upright and in a similar way to modern humans.

THE LIVING ORGANISM: HOMININS

Australopithecus aferensis was a species of hominin that lived in East Africa from about 3.7 to 2.9 million years ago, a period more than twice as long as our species, *Homo sapiens*, has been around. These hominins had ape-like features and chimpanzee-sized brains. While they walked on two feet, they still had long, strong arms, adapted for climbing trees. Judging from the wear on their teeth, scientists believe *Australopithecus aferensis* lived on a diet of leaves, fruit, nuts, and roots.

Homo heidelbergensis fossils have been found across Europe and in Ethiopia. The species is named for Heidelberg, a region of Germany where the first fossil was found.

Homo heidelbergensis

ORDER: Primates
FAMILY: Hominidae
PERIOD: Quaternary, 700–200 thousand years ago
SIZE: Average 1.7 m (5.5 ft) height
RARITY: Very rare

The skull of *Homo heidelbergensis* had a more prominent brow and flatter forehead than a modern-day human skull, with space for a slighter smaller brain.

The front teeth are large compared to the back teeth, which suggests our ancestor lived on a mostly meat diet.

HUNTER HOMONIN
Homo heidelbergensis was a direct ancestor of both Neanderthals and our species, *Homo sapiens*. The species lived between 700 and 200 thousand years ago. This muscular hominin was about the same height as modern-day humans and is thought to have been able to make use of fire and wield rudimentary tools, including axes and spears, to hunt big game such as elephants, hippos, rhinos, horses, and deer.

Glossary

algae Simple non-flowering plants

amber Fossilized resin from coniferous trees

arthropod Invertebrate animal with exoskeleton

avian Related to birds

body fossil Fossilized remains of an animal body

calcite White or colorless mineral

canine teeth Pointed teeth, prominent in predators

carbonized Changed to carbon due to heat or burning

cartilage Strong, flexible connective tissue found in shark skeletons and human ears and noses

cephalopod Marine mollusk such as octopus and squid

cetacean Marine mammal such as whale and dolphin

coprolite Fossilized dung

cyanobacteria Microorganism related to bacteria, able to photosynthesize

decapod Ten-footed crustacean such as crab, lobster, and shrimp

deciduous A plant that sheds its leaves in cold weather

diplopodan Miilipede

echinoderm Marine invertebrate such as sea star and urchin

equid Horse or horse-related

exoskeleton Hard outer casing of invertebrates such as arthropods

fossilization Process of animal or plant preservation

gastrolith Stone swallowed by animal to aid digestion

igneous Formed of solidified lava or magma

incisor Narrow-edged tooth used for snipping

index fossil Common fossil used for dating rock it is found in

keratin Protein, the main ingredient of hair, horns, and feathers

larval Immature form of an animal, especially an insect

limestone Hard, sedimentary rock mainly calcium carbonate

mineral Naturally occurring, solid, inorganic substance

mollusk Invertebrate with soft, unsegmented body, such as snail, slug, and octopus

ornithischia Dinosaur group with bird-like pelvic structure

osteoderm Bony deposit forming scale or plate on skin

paleontologist Person who studies fossilized animals and plants

permafrost Land which is permanently frozen

petrification Process in which organic material turns to stone over a long period

photosynthesis Process used by plants to convert sunlight, carbon dioxide, and water into sugars and oxygen

primate A group of mammals including monkeys, apes, and humans

radiocarbon dating Working out the age of organic matter by comparing proportions of radioactive isotopes

rhizome Horizontal underground stem able to produce shoots for new plants

rostrum The beaklike snout of an animal. Also refers to the bony tail of a belemnite

saurischia Dinosaur group with lizard-like pelvic structure

sauropod Large four-legged, plant-eating dinosaur with long neck and tail

sclerotic ring Ring of bony plates around a bird or reptile eye

scute Thickened bony plate found on turtle shell and crocodile skin

sedimentary Deposited by water or wind

shale Soft sedimentary rock formed from compressed mud or clay

silica Colorless mineral

spore One-celled reproductive unit

strata Layers of rock

theropod Carnivorous, often two-legged dinosaur

trace fossil Fossilized remains of a footprint, burrow, or movement of an animal

vascular Relating to plant or animal vessels that conduct blood, water, or nutrients

vertebrae Series of back bones

xylem Woody tissue in plants that transmits water and nutrients from roots